The
BIG Journey

Bold Inclusion for Greatness

Gary —
Continue to explore
the value of diversity.
Thank you!!! — Andrea

Dr. Andrea Hendricks

Purpose Publishing
1503 Main Street #168
Grandview, Missouri 64030
www.PurposePublishing.com

The BIG Journey
Bold Inclusion for Greatness

ISBN: 9781732683273
Library of Congress Control Number: 2018967505

For permission requests, write to the publisher, addressed "Attention: Permissions Coordinator," at the address above.

Bulk Ordering Information: Quantity sales. Special discounts are available on quantity purchases by groups, associations, and others.

For other inquiries address your requests to the author at email: asdr1364@sbcglobal.net

Printed in the United States of America.

Praises for *The BIG Journey: Bold Inclusion for Greatness*

It is my honor to offer praise for Andrea and her book. Dr. Hendricks is a consummate professional who easily and expertly shares her knowledge of diversity and inclusion. She is also a model of how to bring together diverse people for the betterment of society. We have never needed her perspective and passion as much as we do now, in our country and in our world. This world is torn apart by bias (conscious and unconscious) that hurts everyone and results in so much loss. Our political environment has never been so polarized by fear of "the other." A respectful healing is necessary, and this book offers such promise. Andrea has a passion for improving our world — her knowledge can make the difference, and her persistence is our gift. I have known Andrea to be generous with her time and patient with her audiences and stakeholders as she gently brings them an understanding of what is, what can be, and how to get there!

Connie Russell, President,
Connie Russell Coaching & Consulting

This BIG Book comes as a typical crescendo of the wisdom of Dr. Andrea Hendricks, whom I have known and worked with for more than a decade. I have always been impressed by her professionalism and clarity in presenting cultural facts. Dr. Hendricks sets very high expectations for herself in research and in the delivery of cultural facts. Her eagerness to learn and update herself on various approaches to diversity and inclusion transcend the tactics commonly used by most experts in the fields. Andrea strongly believes that diversity and inclusion have their foundation in both cultural and historical perspectives but should be projected toward the future by creating better workplaces and communities. Her BIG Book will certainly leave you with a strong understanding of well-grounded sets of research-based strategies that can be applied to create harmony in any multicultural environment.

Dr. Emmanuel Ngomsi, President & CEO,
All World Languages

Andrea Hendricks is special and a diversity educator to thousands. The BIG Book will be valued. Proud to support and promote it. Salute Andrea for her contributions to the field of diversity and inclusion. Now, does everyone know she has a Doctorate in Psychology and Policy Analysis, combined with her degrees in Human Development Psychology and Mass Communications? Know she can maneuver anytime, anywhere? Wicked smart. Compassion as she analyzes, discerns, and includes. Thanks for all you do for women and the underserved. BIG Book from a large leader!

Edie Fraser, Diversified Search,
Founder and Chair, STEMconnector and
MWM; founder of Diversity Best Practices

I stand in awe of Dr. Andrea Hendricks' honesty, determination, courage, and passion for diversity and inclusion in the workplace. Andrea will push the reader to think differently about how we approach diversity and inclusion today and in the future. By engaging today's leaders, Andrea will get them into the right mindset to champion change and become courageous leaders.

Lori Maher McCombs, Executive Director,
SHRM of Greater Kansas City,
Missouri State Council of SHRM and
Illinois State Council of SHRM

Andrea has provided in her book, an honest, straightforward analysis of how to understand and leverage the concepts of diversity and inclusion within an organization to drive sustainable business results and positively impact the corporate culture. This is a must- read for ALL EXECUTIVES.

Thomas B. Wright, III, Executive Advisor,
and retired Senior Vice President of
Human Resources and Administration

This book is so needed at this time! Bias and in-group favoritism, whether conscious or unconscious, threaten to hinder us from reaching the tipping point when it comes to global, multicultural diversity and inclusion. The global business community needs to keep focused on real and practical diversity and inclusion efforts if we are to keep moving the needle! Dr. Andrea Hendricks is my "go to" resource for diversity and inclusion. Not only is she a wealth of knowledge, but she applies a practical, common-sense approach that comes from having been in the trenches of business leadership for years. Andrea is an intellect, but she is also in the real world with all of us. She is genuine, never afraid to give her honest perspective. I love her direct approach, always mixed with a sense of humor.

Amy Leslie, CEO,
Perspective Consulting

Andrea is a leader's leader in championing diversity and inclusion in all aspects of her personal life, organizational advancement, and community development. Her "heart and hands" are SO uplifting to serve others as she walks the talk of embracing those around her to be their very best and to meet people where they are. I've had the pleasure to know Andrea for several years and inspired by her abilities and talent to engage and encourage individuals and teams to truly believe they can be their best no matter what their background, circumstances or hurdles in life.

Andrea is a mentor to many and coaches those around her to strive to use their God-given gifts to make this world a better place in spite of the uncertainty we all face daily. I am honored and humbled to call Andrea a friend and confident the book will be an inspiration to many including me.

David Byrd
Natonal Executive Leader
YMCA of Greater Kansas City

Table of Contents

The BIG Cover Story: The Tree

As we journey through this BIG Book, the tree will be the guiding symbol, according to the author, Dr. Andrea Hendricks, and one of her favorite diversity thought leaders, Dr. Emmanuel Ngomsi, who is featured in this book. The author shares that "the tree symbolizes the roots of who you are and brings focus to how the work in diversity and inclusion branches out and flourishes over time to connect to who you are." On her quest of figuring out who she is, an important part of this journey was to figure out her culture, heritage, and ethnic connections — especially from Cameroon, where her ancestors came from. "Finding out your family history is such an important part of finding your purpose, path, and passion." During one of the Urban League national conferences a few years ago, Dr. Henry Louis "Skip" Gates inspired her journey of finding her roots by unpacking a foundational truth that "Until you discover where you come from, you will not be able to fully appreciate where you are going or your purpose and power." One of the author's favorite sayings that is related to the tree is:

Trees stand tall
Trees stand proud
You can go out on a limb for others
Drink water to stay well
Take time to enjoy the view
Remember your roots

— Anonymous

Another great insight that contributed to the cover of the book related to the African culture came through reading the teachings from Archbishop Desmond Tutu. His profound gift over the years has been to share the great work of Ubuntu with others in a big way. Ubuntu is the ability to honor humanity through compassion. It is a South African term meaning "humanity to others"; "I am what I am because of who we all are to others"; "A person is a person through other people." Ubuntu is referenced in many books and training and development sessions across the world.

What the reader should know about the tree is that it is an important custom in the African culture. For years, Dr. Emmanuel Ngomsi has shared his experience about the tree: "When a male child is born in Africa, a tree is planted to honor the birth. However, a deliberate process is followed and significant rituals are performed that lead up to the actual planting of the tree."

First — The tree is pre-selected based on the behavior of the father. In other words, a weak father translates into a weaker species of tree being selected and symbolizes punishing the son for the father's weakness. Conversely, a strong tree is selected when the father has a reputation of good behavior.

Second — The afterbirth, while still warm, is presented to the male elders of the village (they do not attend the birth) as proof of a live birth.

Third — The selected tree, along with the afterbirth, is then placed in a hole; thus, the first food that nourishes the tree is the blood from the afterbirth.

Fourth — As the child grows, he is taught how to go to the nearby creek and get the water to nourish and nurture the tree. The person and the tree are tied together for life.

Fifth — When the person dies, he is buried under that tree. According to Dr. Ngomsi, "When I die, my family knows I must be taken back to Cameroon and buried under my tree."

The significance of the tree is that it teaches us important lessons about responsibility, power, and legacy. It teaches responsibility from the day you are born. It teaches you that you have the power to command a living thing into nature, and the tree continues to be a living testament to the person after death. The tree creates an inclusive interaction between generations, including generations that aren't even born yet — creating intergenerational inclusion. This is significant for where we are today. The BIG takeaway is that we need to recognize that our diversity and inclusion must be nourished and nurtured in our communities and organizations. This is profound symbolism and provides all of us with a common place of reference to embrace and hold on to in our personal and professional lives. The important lessons learned from this journey can be used by all who experience this BIG book.

> *"I cannot exist until I see you, honor you, and see your strengths."*
>
> — **Dr. Emmanuel Ngomsi**

Foreword

The BIG I's have opened my eyes, anew, to legitimate prospects for greatness as it relates to cultural diversity in the United States of America and beyond. In a time — and, literally, a world — of plentiful motivational pronouncements, it is not unusual to hear from writers, and speakers promising success based upon familiar, formulaic, principles and practices. We are often more impressed with these "gurus'" presentation styles than with what needs to be meaningfully researched and substantiated.

Two reasons for appreciating Dr. Hendricks' work are her work ethic and her passion about this work. Before asking others to consider her approach to achieving greatness, she has invested her own great time and energy researching success figures who have tested and applied best practices toward accomplishing desired outcomes. She makes clear that she is passionate about this diversity concept at both a professional level and a sincerely personal level. This passion causes the reader to meet the author at an "I-level," as each "I"-term in her BIG acronyms (e.g., Intersectionality, Interactions, Inclusion, etc.) translates from observational level to personal level. This becomes a very potent self-development tool.

A particular reason for the power of her BIG considerations regarding cultural diversity is the author's ability to marry the personal with the inclusive. She does not allow us to consider one without the other. She would have me (the reader) to know that what I do affects those around me and that the actions (attitudes, aptitudes, alliances, etc.) of those around me affect me. No, this is no epiphany.

We all know that the human condition is reciprocal. But this writing takes us to bigger considerations and understandings. In this case — this *upper* case BIG, if you will — the quest is to find deeper meanings and greater understandings regarding diversity, as we contemplate the inevitability of a continuously evolving multicultural United States of America. Dr. Hendricks helps us to understand that if we are not united, the state of America will lag behind other countries, including those currently considered to be "underdeveloped."

In any measure of "lagging behind," economic factors loom large in that equation. We owe a BIG "Thank you" to Dr. Hendricks for helping consumers of her knowledge, and the knowledge of contributing writers, for considering "cultural capitalism" in a sober and respectful way, as opposed to one that is exploitative and/or mercenary. She helps us to know that an understanding of economic progress requires intelligent study regarding a fluid landscape that is subject to dynamic lifestyles, advancing technology, and many kinds of human interactions — indeed, BIG Interactions — toward greatness.

Contributors to this manuscript have been selected very carefully. The bigness of the subject calls for greatness in those addressing the subject. Even they, themselves, however, would have us to know that greatness should not be thought of as flawless. As Purpose Publishing's Michelle Gines puts it — using a movie title — "The contributing authors give us 'The Good, The Bad and The Ugly.'" Their candor has the redeeming quality of well-learned and now, well-taught, BIG lessons. Let us learn these lessons with minds willing to apply BIG concepts toward achieving big results in diverse, yet, unifying ways. The world will be the better; and, yes, multi-culturally, the BIGGER!

Dr. Carl Boyd—Midwest Hall of Fame Educator and Executive Director of the S.T.O.O.T.S for Boots Campaign (A National Campaign to make US students number one in Academics)

Preface

When I started writing this book, I had a focus and a definite purpose in mind. I wanted to provide a new way of thinking about an old topic that gets batted around on a daily basis, bring my over 25 years of experience with this work to the forefront, share my perspective and viewpoint, and provide a new framework for both newcomers and experienced professionals in the fields of human resources and diversity and inclusion. And finally, my primary goal to integrate my own personal experiences with my favorite resources, stories, books, and research in order to construct a new framework of practice.

My hope is to accomplish what I set out to do over the course of this journey and process. I also discovered the joy that comes from seeing things from a new perspective. Since starting this journey, I have found different dimensions of the diversity and inclusion field and adjusted numerous times many of my informal ideas through readings, surveys, and interviews with colleagues and subject-matter experts' critical reflections, conversations and syntheses of the work of others. The act of discovering new concepts has forced me to articulate new ideas through this writing process that had stayed beneath the surface since completing graduate school.

Through this writing process, I experienced a re-organization of ideas already known, a new approach or framework, and a clear direction on how to maximize programs and services for diverse employees continued success. In addition, the process allowed me, as a diversity thought leader, to relax, relate, and reflect at a whole new level. The BIG book is designed to integrate and embed with other frameworks, case studies, checklists, and resources to continue the practice and encourage the reader to facilitate immediate individual or organizational application. BIG will be successful if the reader absorbs even just a portion of the book and gains or gleans one new concept that they did not know before reading the book.

Here's how the journey began: In 2017, I selected and met with more than 50 professional leaders in one-on-one meetings and small groups to discuss their thoughts and experiences related to diversity. From that group, 25 professional leaders were selected to participate in an online survey regarding the six BIG frameworks. The survey consisted of 10 questions. Then, 8 leaders were selected for a more in-depth, in-person interview to be featured in the book. The varied backgrounds of the research, stories, and interview respondents reflect the truly diverse nature of the diversity and inclusion field and perspective in general and contributed to the successful focus that guided my writing. In addition, my doctoral-dissertation research, which was completed in 1998, sparked interest in this work and was leveraged to provide a solid foundation and a refreshed focus for a broader appeal with organizations today.

My formal education includes training in the fields of educational and counseling psychology along with human development. Additionally, my practical work experience includes human resources, higher-education administration, and diversity and inclusion. The main catalyst for the BIG book centers on those formal experiences. As a consequence, the reader can use the book to spark greater understanding, knowledge, and awareness around diversity and inclusion.

My philosophy reflects a positive or inclusive approach to the topic rather than solely relying on one perspective. Other writers in this field have traditionally focused solely on negative aspects, with no real solutions or impact. This approach seeks to provide a perspective useful for all employees, leaders, diversity change agents, and organizations. BIG will address the audience in greater detail in the next section.

Additionally, this approach is to provide key insights to readers at all levels of the organization. The goal with this approach is to help organizations maximize programs and services for diverse employees' potential so that his or her experiences can increase engagement, satisfaction, and retention over time. The approach suggests that everyone in the organization brings equal commitment to the table and a shared responsibility for producing successful outcomes, next steps, practices, and approaches. In order to accomplish this new approach successfully, we assume that all parties going through this journey will take part in a productive way; and take into consideration the comprehensive needs of the diverse employee, reflecting on the research of Maslow's Hierarchy of Needs.

I have chosen a BIG stance in order to promote a positive learning perspective on this topic. Over the years, there has been a lot of research highlighting concepts, terminology, and practices. However, I will not focus solely on that type of research in this book. Instead, the focus will be on a new framework that maximizes programs and services for diverse-employee engagement, satisfaction, and retention in the workplace.

Audience

As defined by many diversity thought leaders, the diversity practice represents a broad range of ideas and initiatives to create ongoing, productive environments that are safe, inclusive, and equitable and which foster or develop sensitivity to the needs of diverse employees. It is a process and key learning experience that correlates with the ongoing spectrum of diversity focus related to formal and informal activities, programs, and services to enhance the overall engagement, satisfaction, and retention of diverse employees.

The primary audience for this book are employees, diversity change agents, and organizations. The key to success with BIG diversity efforts requires effectiveness from all levels of the organization. As I move into sharing a new approach, this book is designed to encourage strengthening the field of study in hopes of leading to new BIG best practices. I firmly believe the foundation for diversity and inclusion has been outlined for years. There is now an opportunity and responsibility for leaders to move the needle, advance the mission, and share their expertise with others to ensure that diversity and inclusion work does not lose ground over the next 50 years. Diversity must be addressed at both the macro societal level and the micro organizational level, because each affects the success of the other. What are we waiting for? Something big to happen? Big is now or never.

Leaders new to this work will gain insight into the comprehensive nature of the field. Seasoned leaders will become inspired around newer approaches and concepts to share with others in the work-place. In addition, I hope this book will be useful to professionals in other, related fields (such as diversity leaders in supply/procurement) to find practical suggestions for understanding diversity and inclu-sion in a big way, too.

Overview

For decades, across America, leaders at all levels have been sharing their concern about the current state of diversity and inclusion. Professionals in our field have diverse backgrounds, managing diversity and inclusion from within human resources, as consultants, as stand-alone diversity departments/units and in all industries. Although this has allowed us to advance our practice, it has contributed to the perception that we lack an approach to seamlessly and systemically embed diversity and inclusion throughout all industries as a standard of practice. Over the years, diversity leaders have discovered some of today's familiar/ongoing questions about the impact of diversity and inclusion in the workplace that have been asked for decades. How do you define diversity? How do you define inclusion? What is the purpose of diversity and inclusion? How do you advance diversity and inclusion for future state success? The responses to such questions have provided the fuel for debate over the past 50 years as to what diversity should look like.

In Part One, "The BIG Journey," shares the four sparks for the authors interest and passion for diversity and inclusion.

Part Two provides a high-level overview of the BIG history on race and diversity. This history is divided into time periods and provides the building blocks for a shared understanding of how diversity and inclusion practice has been a part of our culture for more than 50 years. And as you look at the time periods, you will discover that the challenges we face today are similar to those that have been confronted in the past. Reviewing history and showcasing how diversity has evolved over the years in America is important. Increasing your historical awareness can help further the field of work and your professional roles. In addition, it is important for us as professionals to view how race plays a significant part of the diversity conversation today. Based on research, our perspectives and approaches in the workplace have been affected by the history of race and diversity in general. If we look at diversity through a broader lens, we are better able to attract, recruit, and develop our employees. Based on our greater understanding and knowledge of the history of diversity, we have been exposed to different approaches that help us increase our capacity and consequently meet the needs of diverse employees in the workplace. Numerous research studies have provided different perspectives on how diverse employees handle engagement, satisfaction, and retention in the workplace.

Part Three describes the authors personal journey toward developing the superpower needed for a BIG journey. Introducing the six frameworks and concluding with descriptions of the four approaches to this work.

Part Four examines the six frameworks in depth and shows how they can guide us toward greater diversity, inclusion, and engagement efforts in the workplace. The BIG framework approach has been chosen because of extensive research and its practical application to diverse-employee engagement in the workplace. At times, we have been more influenced by one perspective than others, depending on what was currently being researched. Now, we are eager to discard old information, research, and past approaches because we often seek to embrace new approaches that work. Based on the research, in order for diversity and inclusion practice to advance and become more effective with retaining diverse employees and sustaining diversity in the workplace, it is imperative for us to leverage a broad range of approaches through an integrated lens. These six frameworks will provide a new, integrated approach to helping address diversity and engagement in organizations.

In Part Five, the final chapter, focuses on the fourth approach — the capability to cultivate BIG across programs and services. When you have leveraged, experienced, and developed BIG, all together, individuals or organizations should be ready to change behavior and navigate to cultivating greater diversity and inclusion actions or efforts. This section will also include a chart of resources the author has utilized over the years in her work.

Part Six is the full bibliography.

Acknowledgements

The timing of this book is around a personal and professional milestone — more than twenty-five years devoted to advancing higher education, human resources, and diversity and inclusion work. There are so many individuals who have helped me with this book. First, I wish to express my sincere appreciation and gratitude to Michelle Gines, CEO of Purpose Publishing, who served as my biggest champion during the pursuit of writing this book. Her expertise, judgment, and support provided the necessary guidance I needed to complete this big project.

I would like to extend special thanks to Dr. Karen Boyd, and Valerie Johnson, my research and compilation team in this work, for their willingness to share their special talents to assist me in accomplishing my goal. Their guidance, patience, and encouragement are the marks of great advisors/counselors.

I would like to give special thanks to my tribe for sharing of materials, experiences, ideas, and listening skills: Dr. Emmanuel Ngomsi, Thomas Wright, Sr., Dr. Michelle Robin, Dr. Keith Harris, Dr. Gerald Hannah, Dr. Karen Boyd, Karen Fenaroli, Eddie Fraser, Kirk Perucca, Carol Taylor, Connie Russell, Lori McCombs, Amy Leslie, Greg Valdovino, Laura Alvarez, Tammy Broaddus, Kelli Wilkins, Debbie Bass, Thornton Shelton, Jr., David Byrd and many more.

Intellectually, I am indebted to my educational mentors from Kansas State University: Soror Dr. Anne Butler, Soror Margaret Kilpatrick, and Dr. Pat Bosco. Dr. Bosco who was my first boss right out of college and one of the best leadership advisors. Early on, their work provided me high engagement around diversity and inclusion and influenced my journey. Dr. Anne Butler and Margaret Kilpatrick, Alpha Kappa Alpha Sorority leaders, ensured that I had the best engagement on campus and in the community while attending college.

Most of all, to my loving husband, friend, and partner who has always been supportive of my choices in life over the years — Terrance Hendricks. His "knack" for always being there and his friendship have been positive influences, both personally and professionally. I appreciate the sacrifices he made and his understanding during this entire process. Thank you for helping me bring a dream to reality. This is something no one can take from you, no matter what happens in life. Thank you for putting me on the right path that, indeed, made a difference, and for your continued guidance and love.

PART ONE

The BIG Journey

"Great diversity is a journey, not a sprint. It is a diversity matrix that elevates over time —1.0, 2.0 to 3.0. Innovative solutions, pioneering, progressive and proactive approaches. Moving from transactional to transformational stages along the way."

— Dr. Andrea Hendricks

Let's take a journey and review where the authors purpose and passion for diversity and inclusion began. During her formal college education, she studied human development, psychology, and counseling. One central focus of her studies was around human behavior. She enjoyed reading and researching how humans behave in certain situations and environments — and the impact of those situations on outcomes. That extensive educational background set up her discovery around three areas over the past 25 years — college-student satisfaction and retention, diversity, and inclusion and employee engagement in corporate America.

First, let's take a closer look at the research she conducted during her doctoral program that sparked the beginning of her journey on diversity and inclusion. This work focused on college student satisfaction and retention. The full copy of Dr. Andrea Shelton's (her maiden name) 1998 dissertation can be found at the University of Missouri system libraries and the Library of Congress in Washington, DC. Below are a few excerpts from the research on adult learners' level of satisfaction with programs and services at a higher-education institution that today links directly to her passion for diversity, inclusion, and engagement programs in organizations.

The First Spark on This Journey: College-Student Satisfaction and Retention

Since the founding of Harvard in 1636, student retention has been a national concern at all levels of education. In institutions of higher education, they have been confronted with the dilemma of student attrition, either voluntarily or because of influence and motivation from internal or external demands (Pascarella & Terenzini 1991). The attrition problem is not a new phenomenon. The problems related to students leaving college have become a loss to the university, loss of educated manpower to society, and, worst of all, personal failure to the student. Attrition had not been perceived to be a serious problem because many students may come back to school or transfer to another institution (Pascarella & Terenzini, 1991). Along with the retention concerns, college students' satisfaction with the collegiate environment has become an important topic for many campus administrators (Astin, 1987). Adult-student attrition is a difficult concept to define because the students' reasons for attending college and their attendance patterns are highly individualistic.

> We must restore our belief in community and the ingenuity and richness of solution building that we all possess. We all have the capacity to grow and contribute, if only we would recognize and value ourselves and each other.
>
> — **Dr. Karen Boyd**
> **Executive Director**

2

Attrition is often defined by the researcher, college, or university collecting the data as the failure to complete a course of study within a specified period of time. Given more time, the students may be able to complete their course of study and be very satisfied with their environment.

Educators place high importance on the individuals who are pursuing a degree, suggesting that completion of that degree in four years is extremely crucial. But with today's economic and social conditions, the completion of a degree in four years is almost impossible and is not a great indicator of one's success of failure (Pascarella & Terenzini, 1991). A demographic change is taking place in American society. The average college student is getting older. Adults are the fastest-growing segment of all population groups in higher education. The number of older students on campuses is expected to continue to increase for the foreseeable future. Colleges and universities are beginning to comprehend the implications of such an increase in their adult-learner population. Adult learners bring a different set of needs and expectations to the campus, and many institutions are beginning to respond to those diverse needs (Lerner & King, 1992). Having focused for so long on satisfying the needs of traditional-aged students, institutions of higher learning now find themselves attempting to direct more of their college services and programming efforts toward adult learners. Since adult learners are a new majority in higher education, many campuses are trying to mold existing services to accommodate this growing market. However, the transition of services provided for this new majority population has been slow to take place. For some college campuses, nontraditional students present major challenges. The wide diversity of characteristics and needs among students makes them difficult to reach with information and services (Streeter, 1980). Data at the national level have indicated a variety of reasons why adult students drop out of college. Students leave for academic, personal, environmental, financial, emotional, and psychological reasons.

3

Adult learners have been forced to absorb the difficulties as associated with being nontraditional students on campuses designed for traditional students. Schlossberg, Lynch, and Chickering (1989) feel that numerous modifications and additions to the typical programs for students should be examined. Adults in contemporary society are functioning within an increasingly complex, interconnected, rapidly changing environment. In order to better understand adult students, educators should be knowledgeable of the various social, economic, and cultural aspects of those adult students they serve. Understanding adult students' involvement (engagement) with campus services will be useful and beneficial for general purposes to assess students and their satisfaction with their environment.

Nationally, student retention continues to be an important concern among college and university officials. Dropout research (Astin, 1993; Tinto, 1987; Noel, Levitz & Saluri, 1985) reveals that students attending two-year postsecondary institutions persist at significantly lower rates than students enrolled in four-year institutions. A model of attrition and retention (proposed by Spady, 1970, and adapted by Tinto) proposed that student characteristics and college experiences interact to affect the decision to stay or drop out. Chickering (1974) devoted an entire study to the differences between residential students and commuting students. His results show that residential students are more likely to persist and are more likely to be involved in campus activities, services, and programs than commuter students — who largely attend community colleges. Schuster and Coil (1982) also supported Chickering's research and indicated that residential students are more likely to become involved in the academic and social life of the campus. They concluded that attending a residential college or university does make a difference in student development as opposed to a two-year commuter institution. Adult learners comprise an increasingly greater proportion of the college-student population, especially at two-year institutions. These older students differ from traditional college students in significant ways, including their stages of development in life, value systems, outside responsibilities, and

> *We are at the point of flushing out the underbelly of our societal norms and realizing that we have much work to do.*
>
> **— Dr. Michelle Robin**
> **Chief Wellness Officer**

learning characteristics. Few studies have advanced the discussion of adult-student involvement with campus services and satisfaction with those services. Having acknowledged that satisfaction is a concern, an institution must be prepared to address the question of how to increase or maintain enrollments. Without a stable enrollment, the institution will experience a reduction in important programs, services, and tuition.

Research at the community-college level offers increased insight into the problems affecting adult learners' satisfaction with the campus environment. Researchers have investigated student satisfaction and dissatisfaction with the college environment and found student satisfaction to be one of the most important indicators of students' attitudes toward their educational experiences (Astin, 1984, 1993; Pascarella & Terenzini, 1991). In addition, the research indicates that student satisfaction with the college environment at any institution increases the likelihood of persistence (Astin, 1984, 1993; Pascarella & Terenzini, 1991). The theory of student involvement evolved from a longitudinal study of college dropouts that sought to identify factors in the college environment that affect a student's persistence in college. The student-involvement theory is defined as the amount of physical and psychological energy that a student devotes to the academic experience. An important element that seems to be missing from the community-college sector is the ability to connect adult learners to the environment through a variety of services and programming designed to promote student involvement and integration. Community college students may be enrolled part-time, work full-time, have family obligations, and be considerably older than the traditional-aged students. In order to foster student interaction on the college campus, special consideration in designing and developing services and programs may be warranted.

It has been considerably difficult for some community colleges to encourage adult students to participate and engage fully in their campus environment. Research continues to indicate that student involvement is a key factor in students' persistence and satisfaction with college life. It will become increasingly important for community colleges to begin to address student-involvement issues and provide interactions on campus which will lead to students developing a since of belonging and enhance the students' total experience on campus.

> *A variety of participants working harmoniously and successfully towards a common goal leads to greatness - Greatness for the individual, greatness for the team, greatness for the organization.*
>
> **— Dr. Emmanuel Ngomsi**
> **President & CEO**

The author conducted extensive survey research on students who were adult learners attending a major college between 1993 and 1996. Her analysis focused on investigating the relationships among adults' involvement with programs and services and their level of satisfaction with services on the college campus. Those surveys focused on a variety of issues relating to the college experience, including how satisfied students were with the campus services provided to the students. In 1993, 9,903 students had completed and returned surveys to the college. Students of all age groups responded to the surveys, however, only students 25 years of age and older were included in this research project. The respondents over the age of 25 represented 57% of the total survey population (N=5,657). Four variables were examined to determine the relationship between involvement in campus programs and services among adult learners, and the relationship between specific demographic characteristics (gender, ethnicity) and ratification with campus programs and services of non-adult learners. According to this research, student involvement is based on whether survey respondents in the sample indicated they did or did not use each campus service. Satisfaction was based on a Likert lowest-level and highest-level scale. The results of this study provided guidance to colleges that want to improve programs and services for adult students. The results for this study concluded that:

- Student involvement and engagement is key to overall retention, engagement, and satisfaction.
- Adult learners present some major challenges for colleges whose programs and services have been geared toward traditional-age populations.
- Adult students, regardless of age, need to have assistance available to them. The relationship between involvement with services and gender, age, and ethnicity does not necessarily mean ratification with the services.
- Non-traditional students, adult women, and minority students need to have programs and services which assist with academic/career support for success.

Some colleges have an especially difficult time retaining adult students. The findings of the study conducted contributed to our knowledge concerning the factors the affect the persistence of adult students attending that college. However, it is evident that in order to increase retention, colleges must encourage adult students to get involved in the campus environment. A student who is satisfied with the campus environment is more involved in the college experience. With increased involvement, satisfaction, and interaction, retention rates should also increase.

Review of the literature suggested that satisfaction of adults may be dependent upon such independent variables as their involvement in programs and services, gender, and ethnicity. In the beginning of this work, only limited research regarding the factors affecting adults learners' involvement with services and satisfaction with services at colleges was available; now, we have seen an increase in this research.

However, additional research with these issues are still warranted for college campuses. The study investigated the relationship among adult learners' involvement with campus services and their level of satisfaction with the campus services. In addition, it reviewed the difference between related specific variables of age, ethnicity, and gender. The research contributed information relevant to understanding the variety of factors associated with adult learners' involvement with campus services at a college. The research provided information to strengthen and improve existing programs and services or create new programs and services to assist adult learners with problems that influenced their level of engagement, satisfaction, and retention with college environments. The research in a college setting sparked her interest years later regarding corporate environments and the diverse employees' engagement with programs and services.

The Second Spark on this Journey: Diversity and Inclusion

The second area that sparked her interest was around the growth of diversity and inclusion efforts in organizations. Between 1998 and 2017, she attended numerous national conferences, workshops, and seminars and continued to review literature on diversity, engagement, satisfaction, and retention efforts. During this time, her focus was to determine whether the same factors for minority college students were applicable to diverse employees in organizations. In addition, she focused on finding any differences between the related specific variables of age, ethnicity, and gen-

Taking a simple process or tool that seems meaningless and make it an added value for the betterment of human life and greatness.

— Dr. Emmanuel Ngomsi
President & CEO

der. As in college environments, this review suggested that diverse employees' satisfaction in organizations may be dependent upon such independent variables as their involvement in programs and services, gender, and ethnicity. No matter the environment — college or corporate — she believes there is still a need for engagement programs and services geared toward diversity because those diverse students or diverse employees persist or withdraw (drop out) at a higher rate from environments for a variety of reasons. Diversity programs and services need to be geared toward how diverse employees leverage the environment, experience the environment, develop in the environment, and cultivate positive outcomes in the environment for success.

From the 1960s to the 1980s, little specific and up-to-date information was available about minority employees in major corporate environments and their level of involvement and satisfaction with programs and services until they started to matriculate to those organizations at a higher rate and with employee engagement and satisfaction surveys/assessments. During this time period, little research had examined whether the link between a perceived positive diversity climate and job satisfaction is stronger for diverse employees. In addition, earlier research and information from key thought leaders about engagement and satisfaction could have been obtained by interviews or conducting more in-depth review of newer existing research or literature. However, such information would have been general, similar to what we already know, and would not have provided an adequate review of the nature of employees' satisfaction and involvement with programs and services. Thus, a need existed to obtain additional in-depth information regarding employees' involvement and satisfaction with programs and services.

As the author reviewed the research findings from 1998 to 2018 on employee engagement, there are potential differences in the relationship between engagement and intent to remain with organizations, even based upon variations in the ethnic, cultural and minority compositions. Research studies revealed that interactions with low levels of engagement, members of diverse backgrounds report a lower tendency to remain with their organization for at least one year than majority employees; at high levels of engagement in the organization, the intent to remain was greater for diverse employees. Research showed that exclusion of diverse employees from engagement programs, processes, services, and career networks became one of the main problems challenging the workforce today. Diverse employees' feeling of exclusion and the inability of their perception of the existence of social support may play a significant role in describing the association between unfavorable experiences of the diverse employees and their engagement level, job satisfaction, and retention rates in the workplace. (James R. Jones, James K. Harter, 2005).

After 2010, additional research continued to look at the effects of race and diversity which examined relationships among race, company experiences, job performance evaluations, and career outcomes for minorities and non-minorities. Overall, diverse employees felt less accepted in their organizations, perceived themselves as having fewer connections on their jobs, received inconsistent feedback and ratings from their supervisors on their job performance and promotability, and experienced lower levels of engagement, retention, and satisfaction. This is a glaring limitation in the human-resources literature considering the fact that diverse employees are more likely to perceive discrimination in the workplace than non-diverse employees (Chrobot-Mason, 2003); (Waight and Madera, 2011). Because diverse employees experience more workplace discrimination, which has negative effects on their well-being, they are likely more aware of workplace policies and initiatives that minimize discrimination. For example, diverse employees are less likely to perceive workplace discrimination and report higher job satisfaction if their employer provided diversity programs and services such as training than if their workplace did not offer it (Waight and Madera, 2011). Therefore, diversity-climate perception should have a stronger effect on organizational equality, equity, and justice for diverse employees.

Today, studies continue to demonstrate that unfair treatment of diverse employees affects the overall engagement, satisfaction, and retention in a workplace. A paper by Jeffrey H. Greenhaus, Saroj Parasuraman, and Wayne M. Wormley titled "The Effects of Race on Organizational Experience, Job Performance Evaluations, and Career Outcomes" investigates the association of diversity practices with an important aspect of workplace well-being, engagement. The authors suggest that association would be mediated by climate of trust and that this mediation relationship would be stronger when employees experienced feelings of inclusion in the workplace. The study reviewed 4,597 employees, and the results indicated that diversity practices are associated with a trusting climate that, in turn, is positively related to employee engagement. Furthermore, the relationship between diversity practices and trust climate was moderated by inclusion. The role of diversity practices and inclusion in promoting trust and employee engagement is a crucial aspect for organizations to leverage, experience, develop, and cultivate over time. The information in this book should provide an approach for human resources and diversity leaders who are interested in improving existing or future programs and services to meet the future needs of diverse employees at all levels of the organization.

The Third Spark on this Journey: Employee Engagement

The final area that sparked her interest was employee engagement in organizations. Employee-engagement programs and services are critically important for promoting greater engagement, satisfaction, and retention for all employees at all levels of the organization. According to Engage For Success organization, "Engagement programs are workplace approaches resulting in the right conditions for all employees of an organization to give of their best each day, committed to their organization's goals and values, motivated to contribute to organizational success, with an enhanced sense of employees' well-being." Examples of employee-engagement programs are mentoring programs, leadership/career development programs, reward and recognition programs, community and volunteer programs, and many more. Many organizations continue to struggle to integrate, embed, or sustain these programs and services within the overall culture for greater diversity accountability and effective results. 41% of managers say they are "too busy" to implement diversity initiatives (Cure, 2016). Some argue that diversity programs aren't increasing diversity in the workplace. In 2016, Dobbin and Kalev discussed why diversity programs fail. They shared that many organizations are basically applying the same approaches they've used since the 1960s — which often make things worse, not better. In the late 1990s and early 2000s, organizations started heavily investing in diversity training and programs after a series of high-profile lawsuits rocked several industries, especially in the retail and financial-services sectors. According to an EEOC

> *Great diversity efforts happen bottom up and top down.*
>
> **— Connie Russell**
> **President**

report, among all U.S. companies with 100 or more employees, the proportion of minorities in management increased just slightly from 1985 to 2014. White women saw bigger gains from 1985 to 2000 — rising from 22% to 29% of managers — but their numbers haven't moved much since then. In the technology industry, while many firms state the need to increase diversity for internal and external business-imperative reasons, most high-level tech jobs remain dominated by white men.

Over the years, research has indicated that diverse employees are particularly vulnerable to high attrition in organizations. A 2008 report by Price Waterhouse Coopers found that, although men and women are hired at similar rates in entry-level professional jobs, at higher levels in the organization, the number of women seems to decline. Seventy-nine of PWC's female leaders were interviewed. The research provided a rich perspective and insights on women in leadership positions. And, while employed, many diverse employees require enhanced connections to engagement programs and services ongoing throughout their careers to remain fully connected. Organizations should constantly review programs and services and ensure that there is a clear pathway for inclusion and engagement, especially at organizations that still do not have diversity efforts or have limited diversity present in their workforce. For larger organizations, these types of programs and services are becoming standard features now. However, mid-sized, nonprofit, and smaller organizations struggle due to a lack of dedicated resources or budgets to build capacity in this area. Lack of diversity efforts increases the likelihood of minorities and women leaving the organization and reinforces the perception of certain organizations as revolving doors. Despite the challenges faced, organizations remain central to conversations about diverse-employee success. By keeping diverse employees central to the talent engagement and management, conversations can lead the way to improved programs, practices, policies, improved employee outcomes, and more equitable and just opportunities in the workplace. These types of programs and services lie with the human-resources and diversity-and-inclusion functions of an organization.

Research suggests that engagement programs and services play a critical role in promoting successful career outcomes for diverse employees at all levels of the organization. Until these programs and services are seamlessly embedded in all levels of an organization, this conversation will continue for years to come. These engagement programs, such as mentoring programs, learning communities, employee-resource groups, and other efforts can help diverse employees who are struggling with corporate culture connect to a sense of belonging. A sense of belonging is defined as a human need, feeling that you belong and are valued for your unique contributions. Over time, effective engagement programs and services have an integrated network or approach connecting all people areas of the organization. When seamlessly embedded in a comprehensive way, these programs and services have shown to drastically improve engagement, satisfaction, and retention of diverse employees.

A recent Glassdoor survey (2014) found that two-thirds of employees saw diversity as a positive when making decisions about where to consider pursing job opportunities. Minority groups and the younger generation value the presence of diversity in a workforce. In their eyes, diversity creates and furthers more diversity. According to the survey, diversity increases employee satisfaction and reduces conflict, improving collaboration and loyalty. The McKinsey research around Diversity Matters (2015) revealed that more diverse companies perform better. The most important drivers identified were advantages in recruiting the best talent, stronger customer orientation, increased employee satisfaction, and improved decision-making. Diversity increases employee satisfaction and fosters positive attitudes and behaviors in the workplace.

Workplace diversity increases job and life satisfaction for women and members of minority groups. For minority workers, for example, the boost in satisfaction kicks in when representation exceeds 15% of the workforce. It is hardly surprising that workers from ethnic minorities report higher job and life satisfaction in more diverse work environments. Research has shown that companies who disregard diversity as a component of their business strategy have a higher percentage of disengaged workers. Organizations that effectively capitalize on the strengths of all employees and leverage their differences and unique values have the most engaged employees. In addition, employees with the highest level of engagement perform 20% better and are 87% less likely to leave the organization, according to a survey by TowersPerrin in the 2013 *Diversity Inc.* article "How Diversity and Inclusion Drive Employee Engagement." The article also shared another study by the Hay Group that found engaged employees were as much as 43% more productive.

A 2017 study by Heidrick & Struggles in an article titled "Creating a Culture of Mentorship" found that mentorship is a beneficial and impact practice, particularly for women and minority employees. The study surveyed more than 1,000 professionals in North America about their experience with mentoring. The study further found that companies that have a formal mentoring program in place had a competitive advantage over companies that did not. Formal mentoring creates effective programs and services that provide connections that employees need to feel a sense of belonging at the organization and are extremely important to their career development.

> *Great diversity efforts is a great mix of races and genders working toward the same goal, not against each other.*
>
> **— Carol Taylor**
> **President**

In 2016, another study, the "Deloitte Millennial Survey: Winning Over the Next Generation of Leaders," found that 68% of people with a mentor said they intended to stay with their organization for more than 5 years; just 32% of people without a mentor said the same.

Diversity does not guarantee an inclusive culture. Diversity is the richness of what one brings to the table, and inclusiveness is about a work environment of trust and involvement. In the article "Using Employee Engagement to Build a Diverse Workforce," authors Riffkin and Harter shared a Gallup study published in the *Journal of Leadership & Organizational Studies* that found the employee-engagement elements most strongly linked to perceptions of inclusiveness are "someone seems to care about me as a person" and "my opinions seem to count." Another Gallup research study published in the *Journal of Leadership & Organizational Studies* suggests diversity can be a competitive advantage for organizations that builds the right environment. Engagement and inclusiveness are closely related. Gallup has also found that engaged employees are more likely to say their company values diverse ideas.

Many companies have had mixed experiences in attaining levels of diversity that make a difference. Progress is undeniable, but slow and incremental. One of the most important lessons is that diversity does not simply happen. Rather, diversity at all levels of an organization is best achieved through dedicated programs and services that focus on specific goals. Diversity programs and services are, in essence, a form of change program, to disrupt old habits and routines. However, research into change management has found that change programs have a high failure rate — about 70%. Most efforts stall because those involved — management and employees — do not believe in them or make them a priority.

Successful diversity programs and services have clear objectives and are led from the top (not just the CEO, but the entire leadership team). They foster active involvement from the wider organization and require the infrastructure to actively manage against objectives to hold individuals accountable for outcomes. Diversity programs and services designed to raise the representation of women and diverse employees in organizations face particular challenges with resistance and inertia arising from unconscious (and sometimes overt) biases that can be deeply ingrained in an organization's culture and unknowingly practiced by individuals.

The minority employee-attrition problem is not a new phenomenon. Historically, organizations have been confronted with the dilemma of minority employee attrition, either voluntarily or because of influence and motivation from internal and external demands. The problems related to minority employees leaving organizations have resulted in significant talent loss to the organization, loss of immediate knowledge and manpower, and, worst of all, potential failure to address and capitalize on the minority-employee experience.

Attrition research includes findings from Muir & Li (2014). What are the top factors that drive employee retention? Are there demographic (gender, generation, ethnicity, geography, etc.) differences in these factors that reveal that non-minority employees in organizations continue to persist at higher rates than minorities? In addition, non-minority employees are more likely to be engaged, involved, and satisfied in programs and services than minority employees. Numerous authors and researchers, including minority-employee-engagement experts Wellins, Bernthal, & Phelps (2005), who authored *Employee Engagement: The Key to Realizing Competitive Advantage,* have investigated minority-employee satisfaction and dissatisfaction with the work environments and found minority-employee satisfaction to be one of the most important indicators of minority employees' attitudes toward their overall work experiences.

In addition, the research indicates that diverse-employee inclusion, involvement, and interaction in programs and services at any

> *Great diversity is meaningful difference in culture, race, gender and religion.*
>
> **— Dr. Gerald Hannah**
> **CEO and Author**

organization increase the likelihood of retention. Therefore, a major opportunity for organizations would be to look at increasing the development of program and services, facilitate better diverse-employee entry/on-boarding into such programs and services, and encourage diverse employees at all levels to take part. Industry leaders across all sectors have discovered that it is not enough simply to open the doors to the organization; they must be willing to provide programs and services necessary to maximize the potential of all of their employees. Engagement and retention programs must be an integral part of the organization for a long time to come.

Diverse talent brings a different set of needs and expectations to an organization, and many organizations are beginning to respond to those diverse needs. Having focused for so long on satisfying the needs of majority employees, organizations now find themselves pivoting and directing more and more of their programs and services efforts toward diverse employees. However, this transition has been slow to take place at several organizations. The wide intersectionality of individual cultural needs among diverse employees makes them difficult to reach with consistent programs and services for all. This difficulty is largely due to the challenges that organizations have encountered with providing inclusive work environments for diverse employees and expanding efforts to enhance programs and services to meet the needs of those employees. Since minorities will become the new majority, organizations will need to mold existing programs and services to accommodate this growing talent market.

Today, non-minorities continue to comprise an increasingly greater proportion of the workplace population, projected to be 63% of available talent by 2020. However, the changing demographics share a drastic shift in population beginning in 2020 to 2050. According to the United States Bureau of Labor Statistics projections in 2006, women will continue to comprise 47% of the workforce through 2050, while minority percentages will dramatically increase from 35% in 2020, to 43% by 2040, and 46% in 2050. In terms of gender diversity, women are now hoping to improve their career opportunities through education. A woman is now more likely to have a 4-year college degree than a man (30.2% to 29.9%) according to a 2015 report by the US Census Bureau. This population shift should result in a change in the representation or available pool of talent in organizations. It won't be long before US minorities are not in the minority anymore. Due to projected growth among Asian, Hispanic, and multiracial groups, traditionally underrepresented populations will hit majority status by 2044, according to the Census Bureau. The United States will no longer have any single ethnic or racial majority by the year 2065. (Pew).

According to a 2015 report by the US Census Bureau, Millennials are now the largest generation in American history — and, ethnically, 44.2% classify themselves as something other than "white." The report also stated that, for the first time in US history, a majority (50.2%) of children under the age of five were classified as being part of a minority ethnic group. Diversity is not just about mirroring the country's demographics. It's also about innovation and performance. Companies that exhibit gender and ethnic diversity are, respectively, 15% and 35% more likely to outperform those that don't. According to global management consulting firm McKinsey & Co., the research in "Workplace Diversity" and "Inclusion Gets Innovative" (2017) indicates that organizations with more racial and gender diversity bring in more sales revenue, more customers and higher profits. As the country becomes increasingly diverse, so does the workforce. Neighborhoods are becoming more ethnically diverse and are thus exposed to diverse cultures from around the world. Because of this growth, organizations need to continue to address the growing diverse-employee population with enhanced programs and services.

Diverse employees look for manageable value-add opportunities in organizations. These value-add opportunities are important reasons to enhance programs and services that minorities feel are important and crucial. An organization that provides the programs and services employees need sends a strong message that minority employees matter — they feel noticed, appreciated, and depended upon by their organization. In turn, these employees will become and remain more engaged in organizations. For minorities who often feel marginalized in organizations to begin with, who feel like they are outsiders in a culture of the majority, the need to belong, to matter, is exceptionally important. "Marginality" refers to the degree of success — or lack thereof — that populations have who try to reformulate or assimilate their identities in order to take advantage of opportunities less open to their group. In some of these marginal populations, there seems to be an imposed barrier holding people back from successful assimilation.

One of the concepts most useful in understanding this complexity of inclusion, or ever-changing career lifestyle, of a diverse employee is that of "mattering." A noted sociologist, Morris Rosenberg, coined the term "mattering." It refers to beliefs people have that they *matter* to someone else. In all environments, diverse employees must believe that others *care* about their well-being/success. They

> *Great diversity is regardless of the backgrounds, individuals come together to share common vision or goal. The more diverse the group, the greater the opportunity to perform at a higher level.*
>
> **— TJ Shelton**
> **Sr. Associate Athletics Director**

20

must have a sense of belonging if they are to succeed. If they feel disconnected, they will feel marginal and are therefore much less likely to engage in the organization or be retained in that organization. The ability of the organization to modify existing programs and develop new services for diverse employees will have a positive impact on the organization's ability to attract, engage, and retain diverse employees.

In summary, diverse talent will be entering the workforce in greater numbers. Because of this growth, organizations need to begin to address the growing concerns regarding engagement and satisfaction with the work environment. Historically, engagement programs have been designed to meet the demands and needs of the majority population at many organizations. Organizations are continually facing the challenges and addressing the opportunities of providing an environment more conducive to all employees. A variety of programs and services helps shape the organization's attractiveness to potential diverse talent, as well the ability of the organization to keep them retained in the organization.

The results of her research concluded that similar to the college student research conducted in 1998, diverse employees navigate through a similar lens if diverse programs or services are not present for their success:

- Minority employee involvement and engagement is key to overall retention, engagement, and satisfaction in organizations.

- Minority employee's level of engagement and retention present major challenges for organizations whose programs and services have been mostly geared toward the majority employee population.

- Minority employees, regardless of gender or ethnicity, need to have programs and services available to them in all organizations. Those programs and services must assist minority employees in a wide variety of professional/career advancement areas for success i.e. mentoring programs, sponsorship programs, rotational assignments etc..

BIG is presented as a new framework that must be present now and in the future to bridge the gap in organizations between the challenges with resistance and inertia arising from biases. BIG is about how individuals, leaders, and organizations move the needle in a bold way for greater diversity in organizations. It's about the approach leaders and organizations use to transform from lack of knowledge and understanding about diversity and inclusion toward greater appreciation, behavior, and action. Increased attention is being paid to enhancing engagement programs, services, and outcomes of organizations particularly as they affect diverse employee engagement, satisfaction, and retention. This book and research cited in this book attempt to contribute and provide a new framework to strengthen and improve existing programs and services and create ideas for new programs and services for diverse employees, which may influence their decision to persist longer in an organization.

Part Two

The BIG History

"A great mix of individuals—cultures, races, genders—working toward the same goal—feeling a sense of belonging."

— Carol Taylor

After transitioning from working on college and university campuses to corporations, Hendricks found herself interested in examining the relationship and the impact of engagement on diverse employees in organizations. Is the relationship between diverse college-student involvement or engagement with programs and services the same as diverse-employee engagement with programs and services in organizations? As stated in Part One, Hendricks does believe there is a connection between what a diverse student experiences on a college campus and in the workplace years later. The author shares that one must understand the history of race and diversity to begin to understand the impact on our culture.

The History: Race and Diversity

Diversity has a definite historical foundation within American corporate history. The history of diversity is divided into several stages so that one can examine the role that race relations, civil rights, EEO/Affirmative Action, multiculturalism, and diversity and inclusion have played out in our country and in our organizations. Race, the Civil Rights Movement, and diversity are not the same thing. In order for us to understand how to manage the future state of diversity, we must review these areas separately in the beginning. There is now a sense of urgency in many organizations to launch or fully capitalize on diversity and inclusion efforts to drive its value equation. Organizations are encouraged to ensure their bottom-line results showcase and reflect the comprehensiveness and integration of diversity in their overall strategy (internally and externally).

Sometimes this comprehensive effort poses challenges of how to get started or refreshed. For years, minority-employee engagement, satisfaction, and retention have been national concerns at all levels of organizations, based on what is happening with diversity in our country, communities, and organizations. We are living in different and difficult times. Diverse employees come from a wide range of backgrounds and pursue a variety of career goals. What benefits a diverse employee from one background may not benefit an employee from another background. Organizations must be prepared to address these rapid changes in backgrounds and needs.

One of the best ways for organizations and leaders who are expected to drive results in this area is to reflect on the historical significance of race and diversity to our country and examine the past and current state of diversity before determining how best to evolve future practices. Having that context allows for better perspective and approaches toward intended new outcomes. Since this book is not about the full history of race or diversity, the author believes it is important for the reader to have a solid understanding and increased knowledge about the foundation of the role that race played in this country in order to fully engage with the current state of diversity and inclusion. In this section, the author will highlight significant events that impact this work. The reader is encouraged to review the literature more in-depth on their own regarding these significant events, which describe the construction of race and diversity in America.

From the mid-1600s to the 1920s, the central focus was about race relations in our country. You must begin in the 1600s to fully understand the impact of race in our country. From 1618 to the 1800s, there were major impacts that led to unfair and unequal treatment for many slaves brought to the country. In 1618, the Headright System was introduced as a means to solve the labor shortage in Virginia. In 1619, the first Africans were brought to Jamestown, Virginia, by boat by a Dutch slaver to solve the labor shortage. In 1705, Freedom Dues were in place for all indentured servants. During their time as servants, they were fed and housed. This usually included a small piece of land, supplies, and a gun. In 1790, the Naturalization Act granted national citizenship to a few and excluded many minorities from this process. The Indian Removal Act was signed into law in 1830. This law was in place to remove Native American tribes from their land. Between 1840 and 1900, there were additional acts/laws that have had a profound impact on race and diversity throughout our history. These included the Treaty of Guadalupe Hidalgo (1848), Homestead Act (1862), 13th, 14th, 15th Amendments, Chinese Exclusion Act (1882), the Spanish-American War, and many more.

In the 1920s, as the Great Depression reached its peak, Americans suffered hardships they never anticipated. While the struggle was difficult for everyone, it was particularly harder for minorities. Unlike their white counterparts, who reportedly accounted for a small portion of the 25% unemployment rate, minorities made up 50% or more. It was during this era that diversity took on a definition more prone to exclusion. As a result of being "different," minorities were often the first to lose their jobs, as well as being denied and, in some of the more extreme cases, threatened for seeking some of the benefits offered under the New Deal and relief programs that started in 1933.

From the early 1920s to the mid-1960s, our justice system found itself in the middle of a number of cases based on the right to inclusion. The 1944 G.I. Bill focused on benefits to help armed-forces members and their families with education, housing, and job rights. By 1964, the United States outlawed exclusion based on race, color, religion, national origin, or sex. The Civil Rights Act focused on the historic discrimination that legally denied minorities full rights. The justice system advised employers that they could no longer discriminate in their employment practices. Yet 50 years later, this same justice system finds itself enthralled in cases disputing fair pay, fair treatment, and blatant discriminatory practices. Race relations and diversity have continued to evolve over the past 50 years. Prior to 1975, the focus of diversity was mainly on race and gender.

The History: Affirmative Action and Equal Employment Opportunity

In the 1970s, Affirmative Action began as a strategy to recruit and hire a more diverse workforce. Affirmative Action played a significant role in increasing the number of women and minorities in the workplace. The goal was to level the playing field to ensure equality. In addition, Equal Employment Opportunity (EEO) was put in place to ensure protection from discrimination. EEO was compliance focused and ready to address legal mandates related to employment. The major social movements of Civil Rights and Women's Rights infused these earlier stages. For instance, in fiscal year 2017, the EEOC filed 184 merits lawsuits (the inherent rights and wrongs of a legal case, absent of any emotional or technical biases), including 124 suits on behalf of individuals, 30 non-systemic suits with multiple victims, and 30 systemic suits. This is more than double the number of suits filed in fiscal year 2016. Additionally, EEOC's legal staff resolved 109 merits lawsuits for a total monetary recovery of $42.4 million and achieved a favorable result in 91% of all district court resolutions (2 - EEOC FY 2017 Performance Report, Nov. 2017). However, despite these staggering statistics, America still finds itself attempting to build a case for the value found in diversity.

The History: Multiculturalism

During 1975 to 1985, some organizations shifted their focus toward more multiculturalism efforts. This stage flows from corporate-image and social-responsibility efforts. One goal of multiculturalism was to leverage and showcase how successful minority and gender hiring efforts were for organizations through marketing and branding. Multiculturalism is a term that is similar to diversity, but it focuses on development of a greater understanding of how power in society can be unequal due to race, gender, sexual orientation, power, and privilege. Diversity is the real or perceived differences between individuals. The multiculturalism stage did not expand broadly in most workplaces at that time due to the fact that some organizations felt it was putting the cart before the horse. In addition, corporate image was viewed by diverse employees and communities as external, window-dressing efforts and not full commitment to the internal realities that diverse employees faced daily in the workplace.

The History: Diversity and Inclusion

Today, marketplace realities have represented major shifts from United States focus only to include global focus. In 1985, the focus on diversity and inclusion expanded its efforts, took shape, and connected to the primary and secondary diversity definitions and approaches. At this time, diversity and inclusion efforts began to evolve and address a more targeted strategic process around workforce, workplace, marketplace, and community outreach. This stage continues today in many organizations in various forms who have diversity as a part of their corporate mission, vision, and values. The current state of diversity strategies and stages continues to evolve as organizations try to redefine their efforts to remain viable and relevant related to diverse employee-engagement approaches.

The History: Cultural Intelligence (CQ)

Between 2008 and 2018, you started to see organizations leverage a new diversity stage called cultural intelligence (CQ). Organizations are finding CQ most useful in understanding the future complexity of diversity and inclusion — nationally and globally. David Livermore, executive director of the Global Learning Center and author of Cultural Intelligence Difference (2011), states, "CQ is defined as a person's capability to function effectively in situations characterized by cultural diversity and work effectively across cultures." The ability of leaders or organizations to modify their behavior, actions, or existing programs for greater, diverse engagements will have a positive impact on the organization's ability to attract, engage, and retain diverse employees or clients. As organizations continually face the challenges and address the opportunities of providing an environment more conducive to all employees, CQ helps shape that future state. CQ is one of those concepts critical for success that most organizations have not fully leveraged. Today presents an opportunity for organizations to refocus and respond to the changes and challenges with diversity utilizing CQ. Successful efforts will result in organizations becoming more nimble, innovative, and ultimately more culturally intelligent (CQ) over time.

Finally, if we look at our work through a broader historical lens, we will be better able to serve the future state of our organizations for years to come. Increasing our knowledge and understanding about the history of diversity and cultural intelligence can lead to greater awareness, appreciation, and, hopefully, enhanced behavior and action toward the importance of diversity, inclusion, and engagement in our organizations. With advancing diversity efforts, leaders will discover that some of the challenges we face today and have confronted throughout the ages in organizations are similar to those in the past. Certainly, progress has been made in some organizations but continued focus and action is crucial for moving the needle even further over the next 50 years. Achieving greater diversity results can be delayed if leaders who are accountable for diversity do not have the knowledge and understanding of how history shapes our future state. Once the historical perspective has been understood, leaders can move on to higher stages of diversity impact for greater application in the workplace. Reviewing the history shows that a wide range of diversity stages that provide a baseline for how this work has evolved and also acknowledges a tradition that must be continued in organizations to address an important value in our country.

The purpose of revisiting race, diversity and inclusion, and cultural intelligence history over time is to:

- provide building blocks for a shared understanding.
- describe how understanding history is a critical part of advancing the efforts.
- help colleagues across your organization understand that this work has been a part of culture from the very beginning.

PART THREE

What's the BIG Deal?

"Diversity is rich. Diversity is value add."

— Dr. Andrea Hendricks

The core concept of the author's personal and professional journey around diversity and inclusion is *being bold*. You must be bold to achieve greatness. Bold is about confidence, courageous acts, daring, not hesitant to break rules to achieve greatness, forward thinking. In order to get to greatness you have to be bold in your actions and acquisitions. It is defined by the deeds of leaders who are committed to making a difference. The greatness of a leader is measured by service to others in the community or in organizations. This area must be developed overtime. You must have the head, heart and mind to excite bold greatness in the diversity space. Therefore, several leaders will be featured throughout this book who the author believes has leveraged, developed, experienced and cultivated bold greatness for powerful diversity programs and services overtime. They are superheros-sheros in their own right. Amazing diversity change agents doing amazing work in the space of diversity and inclusion. So, what's the BIG deal? The author will share her four personal steps toward developing the superpower for this BIG journey.

First Step in Developing the Diversity SuperPower

The authors first BIG step toward developing this superpower was experiencing different places, people, and perspectives as she grew up. Born in Texas, lived in Kansas, and now living in Missouri. So, her journey began when she was born in the big state of Texas. Everybody knows everything's big in Texas. So, living in 3 states and 10 cities over her lifetime was truly a stepping-stone for starting her diversity and inclusion journey. Most of the communities she lived in were majority white communities, with the exception of the communities in Texas. She fondly remembers how communities came together and recognized that a great step could be taken by a person connected to bold inclusion and bold interaction for greatness. By living in much smaller communities, she remembered those who relocated to those cities needed to do some adjusting, assimilating, or coping to survive — similar to minorities in predominantly majority campus environments and even in the workplace. To engage at a high level in these communities, they created big interactions that were connected to social gatherings, church activities, and diverse community programs, festivals, and fairs. Those were important, big, and nurturing activities where everybody received an outpouring of support, even if one didn't know that person or was not living in their neighborhood. In most cases, you felt that you were a part of that bigger community — you felt you *mattered*. As she grew up and throughout her professional career, she travelled nationally and internationally for work and for family vacations. To date, she has visited all states in the continental U.S. except for eight.

Second Step in Developing the Diversity SuperPower

Her second BIG step toward developing this superpower was her engagement in clubs and organizations, and on sports teams throughout her educational endeavors including college. In addition, she worked in the diversity office at Kansas State University and was the Black Student Government President. The leadership experiences in college with the student life office were supported and championed by two of the best executive leaders and mentors: Dr. Pat Bosco and Dr. Anne Butler, both of whom were leaders at Kansas State University when she attended college. Both leaders facilitated her growth with accepting diverse ideas, perspectives, and connections. These significant big opportunities opened her eyes to the importance of diversity in a whole new way. So, growing up in a big way was built on social connections and interactions with diverse individuals from all walks of life was the second bold step in cultivating the superpowers needed to build diverse ideas and perspectives.

Third Step in Developing the Diversity SuperPower

The third BIG step toward developing this superpower was following her "True North." The career interests over the years helped draw her into taking on the diversity work to a bigger level that would result in a greater impact — BIG impact. So, although she didn't start out knowing that diversity and inclusion would be her passion or path, she leaned into it as a result of being called to do something bigger along the journey — going beyond where most people who work in the diversity field work from: a compliance focus or more reactive approach. She hopes people will see her, see her body of work on the proactive side of diversity work, as opposed to the reactive realm of today's current practices.

Fourth Step in Developing the Diversity SuperPower

The fourth BIG step toward developing this superpower was that she was raised in a large family that spanned a broad spectrum of professions and industries, such as religious leaders, educators, successful athletes, and business leaders. This was another big part of her upbringing and a big part of defining who she is today. She gleaned high cultural intelligence (CQ) from her family interactions and travels over the years to diverse places and communities.

In 2011, she started using *Ancestry.com* after attending the National Urban League annual conference in Boston. During one of the sessions, Bill Gates and Dr. Henry Louis "Skip" Gates were on a panel together discussing the importance of finding and knowing your roots. They offered conference attendees a free DNA kit and information on how to analyze your family history onsite at the conference. Hendricks took them up on the offer and received her family information within a few short months. According to the report, her DNA matches are: Cameroon, Ivory Coast, Ghana, Haiti, England, Great Britain, Norway, and the Philippines. How's that for high cultural intersectionality and cultural intelligence? In addition, her families (both sides) are multicultural. She was interested in connecting more with her roots. For example, her father's and mother's sides of the family are both large. Her mother is the youngest of 12 children. Gaining insight into her family history and their unsettling generational journey sparked her interest in this work with an innovative spirit to address diversity and inclusion in a bold way. Weaving together all of these BIG steps on this journey was important for professional growth and passion, deeply rooted in diversity and connected to community. The number of professional leaders and ministers in her life — and their passionate conversations around human rights, civil rights, women's rights — coupled with the strong focus on education and the acquisition and application of this knowledge made all the difference in her diversity journey, life and career too.

Definition of Diversity

Based on those four BIG steps in developing the diversity superpower along the journey, the authors definition of diversity was shaped at a young age. It's defining diversity as all dimensions we are made of or identify with in our lives. Diversity is rich. Diversity is a value add. When she thinks about what shaped big, bold inter-actions for greatness while reviewing and analyzing

> *"Different folks from every walk of life walking together in life."*
>
> **— Carol Taylor**
> **President**

several noteworthy books, authors, and journals that addressed key meanings of diversity, those phenomenal authors absolutely advanced her understanding and boldly addressed the comprehensive topic of diversity, which continues to be a growing universal topic.

One author, the late Dr. R. Roosevelt Thomas, Jr. was often referred to as one of the most noted pioneers in diversity manage-ment in the workplace. For three decades, Thomas committed his life to educating, inspiring, and challenging the workforce to look beyond race and gender. He understood that, in order to reach the desired depths of diversity, organizations not only had to have diverse mana-gerial representation but also — in order to be functionally sound in operation — a relationship with the ranks of management. Thomas' greatest challenge was pushing the concept of diversity and inclu-sion beyond the managerial relationship to valued managing styles and concepts, as well as diverse mixtures, including and engaging the stakeholders. As a conceptual originator, author, and educator, Thomas will long be remembered and a constant reference on the subject of diversity. Even as the term itself evolves over the genera-tions, the strategic approach he applied to the workforce landscape has forever changed how organizations seek quality leaders to build companies from within.

One of her favorite resources in Dr. Thomas' book, *Building a House for Diversity*, in which he describes a powerful fable about diversity and inclusion. This story addresses how privilege or bias can shape our surroundings. When the giraffe invites the elephant in, disaster strikes. The house has been designed to meet the needs of the tall, slender giraffe — not the short, portly elephant. The giraffe suggests ways that the elephant might lose weight and thereby enter the home. Meanwhile, the elephant thinks that the house simply needs to be redesigned. This is a telling story about how an individual's position or organization shapes his or her worldview and how to go about seeing a different point of view. That book and the fable will forever be one of her favorite resources for approaching this topic.

> "Different thoughts, ideas, social class, race, gender, age. Coming together for enhanced outcomes."
>
> **—Kelli Wilkins**
> **HR Leader**

After much soul searching and many conversations, she decided to tackle this subject as the result of a conversation about good ideas in a local coffee shop. Somehow, the underlying context leapt from good ideas to *great* ideas. Hendricks began to grapple with the notion that there was yet another level of this seemingly simple theme that even she may not have yet reached. Convinced that she hadn't even scratched the surface she pondered, *"Is there another level beyond good and great? "What is BIG in the context of the greatness framework when we're talking about diversity?"* "Yes, I believe there is another level." "There's *bold greatness*, and it is my goal to define what that looks like within the pages of this book." "Once we take into account all of the research and literature that has been written over the years and what is still being written on diversity and inclusion, I surmised that there has to be a measurable level of questioning that will ultimately lead us to a palatable vision of what BIG diversity greatness really should look like."

Is there something beyond that? And the author believes there is something beyond that level. She has seen it, witnessed it, and hears it on a daily basis. It is called Bold Inclusion for Greatness — diversity greatness. Yet, most people don't pause and really spend time talking about what bold diversity greatness really looks like. We haven't pushed ourselves beyond the social good or striving for the greater good. And that's an important, big distinction between *good* and *great*. The greater good is a fantastic, conceptual statement. However, the greater good focused on a certain, minimalizing viewpoint of the notion of the few as the context for achieving the greater good — such as the greater good for a few women or for the greater good of minorities. This is a narrow, limiting definition of what is possible, of what is big, regarding the diversity equation. Don't get her wrong, she supports this definition wholeheartedly. From personal observation and experiences, it is her goal to expand, dare, and provoke today's professionals because the greater good is just scratching the foundational-level perspective. Every human resources and diversity and inclusion leader in the country has the same basic foundational understanding of the definitions as we conduct our diversity work. Fundamentally, we all hold fast to the basic principle that "it's the right and smart thing to do. Now, we must learn to leverage, experience, develop, and cultivate diversity in organizations in a new BIG way.

> *"Differences are looked upon as strengths."*
>
> **— TJ Shelton**
> **Sr. Associate Athletics Director**

Diversity Superhero

It is her belief that she learned to leverage, experience, develop, and cultivate diversity as a little girl in a BIG way. Hendricks enjoyed watching Batman or other superhero TV shows. After each show, she would have a script ready for her siblings and neighborhood friends to reenact. She often shared stories about not having all the fancy toys that children have today. They used whatever they could to have fun. They had tricycles and bikes for the high-tech cars, blankets for capes, and sunglasses as masks. Hendricks always played the character of Cat Woman because there were very few women superheroes with great strength in those shows when she grew up. Their scripts were dedicated to fighting evil, protecting the public, and battling supervillains." ***Dictionary.com*** defines a "superhero" as a figure, especially in a comic strip or cartoon, endowed with superhuman powers and usually portrayed as fighting evil or crime." The *Merriam-Webster Dictionary* gives the definition as "a fictional hero having extraordinary or superhuman powers; also an exceptionally skillful or successful person."

As she grew up, she continued watching those famous shows and movies: Superman, Spider-Man, Batman, Wonder Woman, The Incredible Hulk, The Bionic Man and The Bionic Woman, Captain America, Thor, Wolverine, Iron Man, X-Men, Luke Cage, and Jennifer Jones, to name a few; one of her favorite movies today is the Black Panther. All of us, at some point in our lives have wished we had superpowers to make things better. she sure did. At some point in all our lives, we've run around the house in a cape or dressed up in your favorite superhero outfit for a social event — or at least thought about doing it. There's just something fascinating about superheroes that captures the imaginations of young and old alike. It's fun to envision how different our country, communities, and companies would be if we developed superhero approaches to diversity, inclusion, and engagement. She thinks people are fascinated by superheroes because, when we were young, we all liked amazing stories of people with superpowers, people who are super in some way — people who are bigger than life. When people get older, many do not give up on wanting bigger-than-life experiences like being a superhero. They want to believe the stories of people who are bigger and more powerful and more colorful than they are.

So superhero stories continue to be a major part of who we are, the human condition. Most people enjoy going to the movies and seeing actors who can do things to make a difference that we can't do and who have powers that we wish we had. We dream of having the amazing abilities that make many diversity superheroes/leaders well ... super. We mere mortals or ordinary folks usually don't think about the implications that having those powers would carry in a world like ours in terms of moving forward with diversity in a big way. Moving beyond scripting neighborhood playtime, Hendricks continued to use her superpowers to lead proactive efforts to ensure that equality, equity, and justice are valued within workplaces and the community at large. She strives to do this with the courage and bravery of a superhero. Superhero/heroic characters are described as courageous, determined, good natured, insightful, motivated, daring, and epic. The actions of this book and the diversity work that are represented in the BIG stories that will be highlighted throughout this book center on those key descriptors mentioned above. She believes it is time for us to become big, bold, and daring with our superhero/shero approaches toward developing new, dynamic diversity, inclusion and engagement efforts.

What Is BIG?

During her quest to understand BIG, Hendricks stumbled upon some powerful quotes and statements. These statements remained stuck in her head over time. She did not really know what they meant at the time. Over the years, she developed a vision for this work which all seems to make sense now. The powerful quotes or statements were: ***"Dream bigger, Dream big, Think big, Make a big difference, Little things are a big, big deal, Go big or go home, See the big picture, Big as life, Big Bang for your buck,***

Be bold, Live bold, Be bold enough to use your voice, Freedom lies in being bold, Boldness has genius, power, and magic, Big ideas, No dream is too Big, doing Big things, Big destinations, Big journey, Big power, Big impact." She used a great resource to fully visualize her efforts. The activity/resource was a diversity vision board. All of these powerful quotes helped to illuminate and motivate her personal journey to connect others in hopes of changing the way others all view the meaning, purpose, and direction of diversity as described in this book.

So the BIG idea is that we can have the power in today's environment to re-capture the true notion from past civil rights leaders and present leaders. There is a more-relevant-than-ever need for a new, big, diverse perspective and the willingness to stand strong to address those big opportunities. There is a gap that we need to effectively close in a big way. We are now more blended, multicultural, and multi-ethnic as communities, as countries, and as a global society. So, the more multicultural and multiethnic we are becoming in organizations, leaders must not lose the power to be big in this work that will lead to diversity greatness. Today, in many cases, we are still seeing majority, monocultural environments at all levels of the organization. Therefore, diversity engagement, satisfaction, and retention efforts are not being consistently developed, designed, or delivered for greater sustainable success.

It was the German playwright Johann Wolfgang Von Goethe who was attributed with saying, "Whatever you do, or dream you can do, begin it. *Boldness* has genius, power, and magic in it." Each step you take on this journey should begin with being bold—begin BIG!!! So, the BIG deal is defined as "a concept considered so important and valuable, driven by an individual or organization of outstanding importance or power to make a profound BIG difference or impact in the area of diversity and inclusion." BIG stands for "Bold Inclusion for Greatness."

"Bold" and "greatness" are defined as "the quality of being great, distinguished, or eminent, contributing to an organization, group, or purpose that is greater than themselves." Others define "bold" and "greatness" by the deeds of people. Hendricks remembers hearing quite a bit from her mother and others as she grew up. "The greatness of a person is measured by service to others in the community or in an organization over time." Inherent in this is the idea that BIG is a journey rather than a sprint. BIG is a conceptual framework with six key areas to organize big new ideas. This framework is used to help people increase their knowledge, understanding, and awareness around diversity and inclusion. This framework has broad application. Just like the superhero concept outlined in the earlier section, this BIG framework models that concept. Hendricks shares that, to have future greatness for diversity and inclusion in organizations — like a superhero — organizations must do heroic acts/deeds, out-of-the-box things; they must design dynamic programs and services in order to move the needle in this space. So in order to be a super diversity hero at that organization, you need a powerful approach that is more exceptional than any power a leader alone could possess, so that you can use that power to accomplish enhanced diversity programs, services, and initiatives. The ability for a leader to do out of the box things in a way that most organizations have been challenged to do in the past is bold, is big, and will lead to greatness. That is BIG!!!

The Six Types of "I"

BIG is designed to explore six designated concepts necessary to build a well-structured approach to help you become bold in a diverse trek toward attaining the future destination of greatness. The six concepts are: Intersectionality, Interactions (diverse), Inclusion, Ideas (diverse), Innovation, and Intelligence (cultural). In today's global society, leaders and organizations must learn new ways to navigate and leverage diversity by enhancing engagement programs and services with a focus on the six "I's."

- *Intersectionality* is defined as "engaging and valuing a full range of diversity dimensions (primary or secondary) in diverse programs and services." This approach supports all of the interwoven diversity dimensions that one encompasses as an individual. Ensuring that diverse programs and services are interlocking and interwoven throughout the organization allows employees to bring their whole self to work. The concept of "Mattering" -Who am I/Who I am- is a critical factor. Over time, leveraging intersectionality will lead to greater engagement in the workplace. You leverage intersectionality by making sure all employees matter and have a seat at the table. The opposite of intersectionality is living and working in a monocultural environment or thinking with a monocultural mindset.

- *Interactions* is defined as engaging in diverse interactions, networks, and connections that are leveraged for success. These diverse programs and services can be between individuals, groups, and teams to build effective diverse relationships. Over time, leveraging big diverse interactions in programs and services between employees, groups, and teams is key to building trust, respect, and appreciation for effective, ongoing diverse relationships. The opposite of interactions is isolation and an absence of trust, which limits our ability to have meaningful relationships and fulfilled lives in the workplace.

- *Inclusion* is defined as the act of a person being included within a group. This approach supports the active, intentional, and ongoing efforts as engaging inclusive programs and services that support a sense of belonging, feeling valued, and feeling

that you matter in the workplace. These inclusive diverse programs and services allow for one to make big investments in
the workplace. Employees have the opportunity to be fully
engaged in the workplace. The opposite of inclusion is exclusion, which will lead to helplessness, stress, low morale, and
employees quitting their jobs at a higher rate.

- **Ideas (diverse)** is defined as people who can see and value
things in a different way. This approach supports the intellectual flexibility to generate something better than one could do
individually as engaging and leveraging diverse ideas, perspectives, and thoughts for greater outcomes in diverse programs and services. There is more than one way or approach
to achieving a stated goal. We must focus on new intentions,
breakthrough concepts that result in a sustainable competitive
advantage. Leveraging the best outcomes of others' diverse
ideas ensures that others' opinions are free from bias, blind
spots, or filters. The opposite of diverse ideas is "more of
the same" — staying in a rut or sticking with traditional
practices and processes. Over time, this will limit our ability
to generate new and different paths to greatness out of fear of
failure or accepting others who have different points of views.

- **Innovation** is defined as unlocking in an environment to create
out-of-the-box ideas and perspectives from diverse individuals. This approach supports fostering experiences as engaging
greater creativity for diverse programs and services. Diverse
employees need diverse programs and services that offer varied experiences and perspectives in order to fully contribute
in the workplace. Over time, these innovative programs and
services must be utilized to drive value creation, new ideas,
new methods, and better solutions, ensuring realization of the
greater good for all. The opposite of leveraging innovative

diverse programs and services in the workplace is what we have seen for many years. Over time, organizations that are doing the same thing, stuck in a rut, not willing to change, and using only traditional approaches to programs and services will see greater/higher attrition, dissatisfaction, and low engagement.

- *Intelligence (Cultural)* is the capability to relate and work effectively in culturally diverse situations. This approach supports the measuring a persons capacity to function effectively in a multicultural environment as engaging and interacting across cultures in the workplace (in diverse programs and services) with individuals who are different from you. Overtime, if leveraged correctly, cultural intelligence will enable us to adapt effective interactions across cultures to gain new insights and develop better initiatives in the workplace. The opposite of cultural intelligence is monoculture, nonculture, or living an unenlightened life. We choose instead to live in a vacuum that is void of exposure or experience with other environments or cultures. We limit our ability to walk in the shoes of others or empathize with conditions or issues that are outside of our own cultural context. Over time, we will not be able to develop relationships beyond our immediate, familiar circle, thus preventing us from benefiting and learning from others. Personal and professional growth will be stunted.

The "I"s Have It

Hendricks shared that during a working session on research, understanding and compiling data for this book, one of the publishing team members shared that not everyone has broad exposure to diversity and inclusion concepts or approaches on a daily basis. Valerie Johnson, research team member, an ESL instructor and a college and career coordinator, had an "Ah, ha!" moment.

She realized that she had the same limited perception of diversity as most others — was just about a look, different people of color, races, and recognizable cultures. Her perception about diversity touched only the primary dimensions of diversity not secondary dimensions or even taking into consideration the intersectionality of a person. Once she began to research diversity, she immediately broadened her definition and perception of diversity, which led her to an understanding of the plight of those trying to incorporate true diversity into our culture, communities, and companies. Her primary goal as an instructor is to assist adult students in learning to speak English and to transition them into the American culture. According to Valerie, many of these adult students encounter biases when they start assimilating into American workplaces and communities. Her research on diversity and the six "I"s, as outlined in this book has helped her to better understand the challenges people still face on a daily basis. In addition, understanding the six "I"s has equipped her to help adult students to have a sense of value as they enter the workforce. The concept of BIG is more relevant than ever before, given the "Black Lives Matter" platform, the "ME TOO" movement, and the focus on immigration and other diversity-related areas, which have all seen an uptick over the past few years. For her, the "I"s have wide appeal beyond the workplace and those professionals close to her work. Valerie views using the "I"s to also help diverse individuals transform their lives as they navigate this complex world. This too is BIG!!!

Four BIG Approaches

There are four approaches to the six "I"s. When putting the "I" words together, BIG is the capability to leverage, experience, develop, and cultivate across individuals and organizations in search of a BIGGER vision or goal for enhanced diversity engagement programs and services. These four approaches are defined next.

Leveraging BIG is the first approach. When you first determine you need a bigger impact for your diversity and inclusion efforts, it is easy to move toward finding a quick fix or solution. One solid approach is how an individual or organization leverages the BIG "I's for a bigger impact. One has to determine how they will leverage and navigate the power of their past and current diversity investments to be bigger than before and to maximum advantages with existing key resources, programs, and services. Leveraging BIG is the ability of people to influence their environment in a big way that multiplies the outcomes of their efforts without necessarily creating a need for increased resources.

Experiencing BIG is the second approach. When the necessary resources have been leveraged for bigger impact for your diversity and inclusion efforts, it is still possible not to experience high engagement opportunities. One solid approach is how you experience the BIG "I"s all at the same time for a bigger approach. Experiencing BIG will help break past patterns and lay the groundwork for the new bigger future diversity understanding, knowledge, skill, or practice, with everyone's direct observation and participation in diverse programs and services.

Developing BIG is the third approach. When the person or organization has leveraged and experienced BIG, they are developing the power of their own personal growth toward greater awareness and appreciation for diversity and inclusion. This is where a person or organization becomes more mature, advanced, and evolved for greater effectiveness around diversity and inclusion. Developing in and around diverse programs and services with other people from a variety of groups widens the personal, professional and organizational circles.

Cultivating BIG is the fourth approach. When you have leveraged, experienced, and developed BIG — all together — you or the organization should be ready to change behavior and navigate to cultivating bigger diversity and inclusion efforts. This level is the action oriented approach. This only comes when you or the organization expands the capacity for viewing diversity challenges from multiple perspectives or vantage points and has the willingness to do something about those challenges. This approach is not about cultivating the environment through a single filtered lens, but expanding ones views and considering multiple options when making key decisions that impact others.

The author believes that the six BIG "I"s concept and the four approaches can serve as the framework to bridge the gaps with organizations, leaders, and employees to reach a future state of diversity, inclusion, and engagement.

PART FOUR

The BIG Deal

*"All of the dimensions we encompass as individuals –
being open to seeing how our individual and collective
dimensions connect with one another is the superpower
of effective diversity."*

— Dr. Andrea Hendricks

Hendricks BIG is the framework for this book. It applies to leaders and organizations on the journey toward diversity greatness. The content as developed here will be presented to you in the form of the six "I's" on this diversity journey; they are explained, examined, and essentially used as a new diversity strategy to achieve bold greatness regarding engagement with programs and services for diverse employees in the workplace. This is how individuals can navigate their own personal or organizational introspection for future direction toward a new diversity approach in the realm of BIG. It's Bold Intersectionality, Interactions, Inclusion, Ideas, Innovation, and Intelligence for Greatness. It's not one area, but all six areas combined together, working together, understood together, and navigated together to achieve the highest dimension of personal or organizational success. It's the next big expository on diversity.

Next, each one, as defined, will be shared and demonstrated through the lens of LEDC: Leverage, Experience, Develop, and Cultivate connected to BIG. We have taken a look at the approach of how we got here. Now, we are ready to look at a new framework for effective, practical application of this work. As you begin your journey toward "greatness," the author encourages individuals and organizations to explore their own diversity stories and experiences in each area. Once you determine how to leverage the "I's" and examine how to leverage your personal or professional experiences to increase your current status, she challenges you to review how you have developed the "I's" — moving from the lower end of the "I" spectrum toward the higher "I" place. This will challenge you and push your personal boundaries toward "boldness" in taking steps to cultivate changing the world around you through sharing and utilizing stories, tools, exercises, and implemented activities. Continuously cultivating BIG will allow you to acquire the knowledge needed to sustain yourself or organization as an integral contributor in the realm of diversity.

We have selected the "superhero/shero" approach to add some excitement to this journey. Superheroes may be a form of escapism, but, like stories of any kind, they matter because they allow us to connect to other people. With the superhero concept, one is trying to have some sense of control in a world where one feels powerless. With most superheroes, it's the desire to do the right thing, the idea of lost culture, being a good person — they are and always have been great stories of hope. In each chapter, you will meet several superhero/sheroes that the author believes have cultivated hope and made the right investments to help advance diversity and inclusion in their own way and in a BIG way.

Diversity is not something that exists in a vacuum. Like the air one breathes every day, it is ever present, with variations in quality. Diversity is, and should be, something that is measured against other things with similarity. The ultimate goal of creating diversity in the world in which you exist is to find and elevate uniqueness to a degree of excellence where the world can't help but take notice. Because diversity should become a distinctive attribute found in the people who make up an organization or group, it will become more evident as you cultivate both an environment and overall consciousness in your organization or group. Every "I" must become a daily, deliberate cognitive-development process. Let's take a look at each one in greater detail.

BIG Intersectionality

"Intersectionality is recognizing the many facets that all of us bring to the table when approaching a project or problem. Embracing intersectionality rather than ignoring or dismissing the potential impact. The result is often greater understanding of others and an appreciation of what shapes one's worldview."

— **Dr. Karen Boyd**

Leveraging Intersectionality

The first BIG "I" the author believes individuals and organizations should leverage for enhanced diversity and inclusion programs and services in the workplace is an Intersectionality mindset and approach. Past programs and services have not leveraged intersectionality as a way to bridge the gap with diverse employees. Most programs continue to isolate individuals' diversity dimensions rather than integrate them seamlessly into the organizational culture. But what does that even mean? How do we leverage an intersectional approach to make equality "real"? We defined intersectionality as "the acknowledgement that our social identities overlap and intersect and form new, more-specific identities, with new implications. In addition, intersectionality is defined as the ability to engage and value a full range of diversity dimensions — primary dimension and secondary dimension — for success. The author begins this journey with intersectionality because she believes individuals and organizations need to spend time leveraging the "whole self" paradigm to be effective in reaching greatness before they can leverage inclusion, diverse ideas, or innovation in the workplace. You must know who you are and then be allowed to bring your whole self to work and have programs and services designed to effectively support who you are, so that you can be great in your intentions and interactions. Until work environments allow for intersectional engagement experiences with diverse employees, they will lose major key drivers of success related to productivity, satisfaction, and retention.

This framework supports all of the interwoven diversity dimensions that one encompasses as an individual. Ensuring that diverse programs and services are interlocking and interwoven throughout the organization allows people to bring their whole multidimensional and multi-cultural self to work, and that is important. The author believes intersectionality is connected to "Mattering." How a person matters in the workplace is important. Mattering means that an individual contributes in a unique way, feels that they can make a difference, and are contributing to the greater good of the organization. "I am seen, acknowledged for my talents, and appreciated." It is also connected to a strong concept of "Who am I?" and "Who I am."

> *Great efforts of diversity will help all people appreciate the similarities, differences, nuances, and cultural pillars to create better products, make less subjective decisions in hiring, think 'who's not at the table that should be' and produce better leaders.*
>
> **— Laura Isabel Alvarez**
> **Consultant**

Over time, leveraging intersectionality will lead to greater engagement in the workplace. According to author Christine Comaford in her book *Power Your Tribe*, "There are three things that humans crave: safety, belonging, and mattering. No matter where you start, where you're going, or how you get there, individuals need these three things for the journey." Maslow's "Hierarchy of Needs" has been shared as that foundation for this work for many decades. Maslow's work showed that, before individuals seek self-actualization, they must feel safety, belonging, and mattering. Without these, individuals cannot perform, innovate, feel emotionally engaged, or move forward. The opposite of intersectionality is living and working in a monocultural environment or having a monocultural mindset. Over time, this will lead to greater isolation and a lack of appreciation of the various dimensions of the whole self and its collective power to impact greatness and productivity. You leverage intersectionality by making sure all employees matter and have a seat at the table. One of the author's "go-to" national diversity leaders is Dr. Shirley Davis, author of *The Seat*. She outlines the steps necessary for diverse employees to gain a seat at the table in organizations. "A seat at the table" means an individual has a voice, visibility, and an opportunity to connect to the vision of the organization.

Experiencing Intersectionality

Many generations found themselves upholding the Three Musketeers' motto of "All for One and One for All." The concept was simply, "When you mess with *me*, you're messing with *three*." The challenge in the early years, and even more so now, was that "one" consisted of a fraction of many — many beliefs, many cultural practices, many races, many social attitudes; the list continues. Far too often, we found ourselves having to choose one fragment of who we are over another in order to be included, in order to interact, or even in order to be valued enough to exchange ideas. Even the Pledge of Allegiance to our country requires us to be "Indivisible, with liberty and justice for all." "Indivisible" means "unable to be divided or separated into parts; incapable of being divided." Indivisibility is the direct opposite of Intersectionality. As a nation, we struggle with the ability to accept the "whole" individual — the sum of the parts of the person. As globalization introduces people to new traditions, multiple cultures, blended families, and non-gender-oriented concepts, we find ourselves struggling to maintain simplicity in our relationships, our communities, and in our workplaces.

Intersectionality is all of the dimensions we encompass as individuals. We all experience intersectionality because we all have primary and secondary dimensions of diversity. Being open to seeing how our individual and collective dimensions connect with one another is the power of effective diversity. We have more in common with one another than ever before. Embracing the way we intersect with one another can facilitate how we discover more common ground. Intersectionality is an analytical framework that attempts to identify how interlocking systems of power impact those who are most marginalized in society. Intersectionality considers that the various forms of what it sees as social stratification, such as class, race, sexual orientation, age, disability, and gender, do not exist separately from each other but are complexly interwoven. While the theory began as an exploration of the oppression of women of color in society, today the analysis is potentially applied to all categories.

Civil Rights advocate, sociologist and law professor at UCLA and Columbia Kimberlé Williams Crenshaw coined the term "intersectionality" in 1989, and it's a buzzword for activists, academics, and diversity and inclusion professionals. All it really means is exactly what you're probably thinking — our social identities overlap and intersect and form new, more-specific identities with new implications. The individual identity groups we belong to — race, class, ethnicity, religion, gender, sexual orientation, nationality, etc. — do not exist in a vacuum, and they cannot be compartmentalized. Intersectionality acknowledges that a person can simultaneously belong to multiple historically marginalized groups. The elements are inextricably linked, and all aspects of identity are integral, interlocking parts of a whole. Crenshaw states that intersectionality draws attention to "invisibilities" that exist. In her earlier work, she discusses intersectionality as it relates to women — the invisibilities that exist in feminism and the impact of systematic oppression.

According to intersectionality, the context and degree to which we experience power or marginalization is influenced by the intersection of our varying identities. Those who are part of multiple non-dominant groups may be more sensitive to and aware of their differences, and are perhaps uncomfortable colluding with the cultural "rules" of the dominant group that are unfamiliar.

Intersectionality theory states there are implications to overlapping marginalized identities, but intersectionality also acknowledges layers of privilege. Being a part of multiple non-dominant groups — Black women, LGBTQ people of color, disabled people in poverty, etc. — creates layers of barriers to equality and justice in the same way that having multiple dominant identities — white, male, Christian, able-bodied — creates layers of privileged possibility.

Intersectionality as a practice has the potential to develop more common ground, creating more opportunity for inclusion. If people allow themselves to all of them at once, there is a greater possibly they will meet someone who can relate to some point within their web of identities. It's as simple as saying, "Hey, I may not understand all of what it means to be them, but I can relate to this one thing, and that's a starting point. All you need is a starting point to connect with others.

Intersectionality has become a buzzword in the diversity, equity, and inclusion space. While the theory has been used in the academic and social-justice context for some time, it has gained more traction in corporate diversity and inclusion practice over the past 10 years. Organizations like Twitter have been intentional in using intersectionality as part of their diversity leaders' title and common language around diversity in general, affirming the need to create space for and see employees as their "whole selves." There have been studies that create the case for organizations to replace traditional diversity and inclusion efforts that subscribe to a "check one box," monolithic approach to difference and identity with programs and strategies that take into account the complex nature of our intersections.

> *It is the blending of people and ideas.*
>
> **— Dr. Gerald Hannah**
> **CEO and Author**

Developing Intersectionality

What does intersectionality "look like" in practice? One of the biggest challenges to developing intersectional, equitable solutions is not having the quantitative insight. For the most part, our level of inquiry into diversity and inclusion areas of opportunity has traditionally been one-dimensional. For example, many people solicit demographic data when conducting focus groups or engagement data, but more often than not, the demographic questions do not take into account the intersections of identity. So, whereas we may be able to analyze the experiences of men or women, or people of color, we miss the opportunity to understand the experiences of women of color, men who may also have a disability, Latina Millennial women, or Asian male leaders — all critical intersections that inform the workplace experience.

While it might seem intuitive, this level of inquiry requires intentionality and is requisite to beginning to identify equitable solutions for workplace environments. In any development or engagement effort, there will be assumptions that individuals and organizations make when designing or delivering significant programs. The point is to start with discussions around intersectionality right out of the gate. Ask the question: How can you and your organization be more intersectional in your approaches toward inclusion and equity? For instance, the experiences of Black and Latina women are significantly different from those of white women. Organizations must continue to be intersectional in their approach, actively centering the engagement experiences of those employees who have typically been at the margins of diversity and inclusion efforts. Organizations must continue to tailor solutions that consider the complexity of the "whole self."

Bold Intersectionality for Greatness is the ability to remove the socially accepted mistreatment of individuals based solely on their social-group identity. It is the willingness to embrace our differences and dare to interact within a diverse environment for the purpose of cultivating an infrastructure for a common vision that is bold enough to make decisions that defy societal rules for who we should or should not be. Simply put, Demetria Miles-McDonald, Founder of Decide Diversity, wrote, "Intersectionality occurs when a person identifies with two or more minority or marginalized groups." She explains, "There is no limit to the number of minority groups a person can belong to, but the more marginalized groups a person identifies with, the more difficult it is to explain her or his experience."

The challenge with addressing intersectionality is that the experience in and of itself is difficult to define. If it is hard to identify the specific experiences one has, intersectionality becomes an experience for which it's difficult to find the educational and career attributes needed to develop a reference point for evaluating its relativity to your personal and professional vision. For example, we can't deny that we exist in a society that still pigeonholes women in the more nurturing workforce roles such as nursing or childcare. This display of intersectionality creates the perception that there's something fundamentally wrong with a man seeking a career as a nurse, instead of as a doctor, or becoming a childcare provider as opposed to a childcare administrator.

Today, Crenshaw continues to shed light on the inequities that exist on various levels for both men and women, wherever they live. From education to executive boards, Crenshaw continually shares the fact that organizations play a vital role in the development of tomorrow's workforce and the contributions they make to establish the true diversity inclusiveness necessary to make its mark in work-places and the community.

One of the author's favorite resources is a diversity-dimensions wheel. Dr. Hendricks has used the wheel to help employees, leaders, and organizations find and develop their diversity stories. The "Dimensions of Diversity" wheel helps to show the complexity of diversity. Throughout this activity the complexities and assumptions of the model are discussed that we make (usually about the behaviors of other people), which ultimately drive our own behaviors, which, in turn, have an impact on individuals and organizations. The model highlights the "Internal Dimensions" which receive primary attention in successful diversity initiatives. The elements of the "External" and "Organizational" dimensions often determine the way people are treated, through engagement programs and services, who "fits" or "doesn't fit" in a department, who gets the opportunity for development or promotions, and who gets recognized.

Let's take a look at a superhero story about how Dr. Karen Boyd, who is a capacity-building professional and Executive Director of Ivanhoe Neighborhood Association in Kansas City, Missouri, leverages, experiences, develops, and cultivates intersectionality related to programs and services in organizations. Karen Boyd has spent the past 17 years as a capacity-building professional working with diverse communities and populations throughout the Kansas City region. The Ivanhoe Neighborhood Association is among the largest, predominantly African-American neighborhood associations and community development corporations, serving 6,000 residents with comprehensive housing rehabilitation, economic development, and skill-building programs. Over the past 30 years, Dr. Boyd has provided community-engagement and market-outreach training and development for nonprofit organizations, neighborhood associations, and major corporations throughout the United States. Karen Boyd has spent her life connecting businesses and organizations to their customer bases through leveraging intersectionality as a key factor for meaningful success. As a capacity-building professional, Dr. Boyd has focused her current and past work in diversity and inclusion by bringing to the table the varied perspectives and biases of different people and their effect on a particular opportunity or issue. She utilizes these diversity and inclusion skills in her current position, built upon practices and experiences in previous executive roles in not-for-profit organizations and higher-education institutions in Kansas City.

BIG: Intersectionality Story

Dr. Karen Boyd has been leveraging Bold Intersectionality for Greatness for many years. In her bold impact throughout Kansas City, Karen exemplifies the insightful superhero trait through her keen insight and perceptive powers that have enabled her to recognize and embrace the whole self that others bring to the table. By unlocking the value and contributions of the whole self, they identify opportunities, solve problems, and address concerns faster and more comprehensively. Her insightful superpower often results in a deeper understanding of others and a greater appreciation of what shapes one's world view — translating into a more impactful solution or discovery.

In 2003, one life-changing landmark project that was assigned to Dr. Boyd when she was an assistant vice provost for strategic marketing and communications at a major university in the Midwest was a science festival event. The event brought together more 1,000 middle-school girls with more than 100 female STEM professionals. Karen's role was to manage and coordinate experiential programming for students, parents, and professionals that highlighted the diverse and inclusive opportunities available in these fields. The event also provided access to female middle-school students from diverse cultures and ethnicities to come together and have access to highly accomplished female professionals. Dr. Boyd learned firsthand about the impact that such experiences can have on the trajectory of one's life and how such experiences can uncover opportunities that reduce barriers to success. Thus began her focus of utilizing intersectionality as a diversity and inclusion culture-building tool.

As part of this focus, Dr. Karen Boyd has developed an insightful survey instrument that she uses to establish a baseline of perspectives and biases. She shares the Survey of Hopefulness as a best-practice diversity approach that helps people understand their whole self, related to problem solving and issue resolution. Boyd shared that intersectionality, and the Survey of Hopefulness was developed from existing surveys that focused on discovering the types and levels of trauma that impacted learning among teenage students while working at an alternative high school in the Midwest. Her 26-question survey covers a full range and provides a picture of a person's experiences and biases. The survey expanded the focus to professional-development environments as well. The survey has been utilized by over 500 people thus far. Survey results are used to help the individual and others understand how diverse life experiences shape our thoughts, reactions, expectations, and approaches to problem solving.

The concept of intersectionality recognizes that certain individuals face multiple and intersecting forms of environmental and structural experiences — good, bad and ugly. It is based on the understanding of all the dimensions that make up the individual and being open to seeing how our individual and collective dimensions connect with one another. According to Dr. Boyd, "When one pauses to consider how past and daily experiences impact behavior, that individual becomes more aware of these patterns and can conscientiously suspend their impact as they seek to productively interact with other people, particularly those from cultures and backgrounds that are different from their own."

A great quote by Audre Lorde is "There is no such thing as a single-issue struggle, because we do not live single-issue lives." This statement provides context for intersectionality and its strategic role in the diversity and inclusion work space. This is significant due to the increasingly diverse populations served in our organizations, marketplace, and communities. We cannot reach, teach, or contribute without first understanding, on a multi-dimensional level, the makeup, the fabric of our own self, and how that impacts how we show up and interact each day. And recognizing that past conditions and experiences generate big filters, both positive and negative, depending upon shifting relationships and environments that we are exposed to and learn from. Most importantly, this process of building intersectionality muscle in a big way takes time and the willingness to be vulnerable enough to recognize that it is "OK" to be yourself. Organizations need to pause, slow down, and examine perspectives, beliefs, and feelings — and honor their employees.

"Great diversity efforts look like normalized teamwork and productivity across groups, communities, organizations, etc… toward the common good. Great diversity efforts reflect the intentional melding of creativity, idea generation, and solution building across populations." The BIG book provides organizations with the permission to reflect on how they are valuing intersectionality in the workplace. Such permission is long overdue in a society and world that compel us to get smart, be smart, act smart fast. We have forgotten how to pause to refresh and replenish our programs and one's self. This BIG approach provides the new space and tools to understand one another's value by first understanding the whole individual.

INTERSECTIONALITY

DEFINITION OF INTERSECTIONALITY	Valuing a full range of diversity dimensions (primary or secondary). This approach supports all of the interwoven diversity dimensions that one encompasses as an individual. Allows people to bring their whole self to work. The concept of "Mattering" — "Who am I?"/"Who I am." Leveraging intersectionality will lead to greater engagement. Intersectionality making sure all employees matter and have a seat at the table.
POLAR OPPOSITE OF INTERSECTIONALITY	The opposite of intersectionality is living and working in a monocultural environment or have a monocultural mindset. Over time, this will lead to greater/ higher isolation and a lack of appreciation of the various dimensions of the whole self and its collective power to impact greatness and productivity.
LEVERAGE INTERSECTIONALITY	Leverage intersectionality when you bridge the gap between individuals, allowing them to bring the "whole self" paradigm to the table.
EXERIENCE INTERSECTIONALITY	Experience intersectionality when you embrace all of the dimensions that contribute to your uniqueness as individuals. Open to seeing how your individual and collective dimensions connect with one another to harness the power of effective diversity.
DEVELOP INTERSECTIONALITY	Develop your perspective on intersectionality by realizing that you have more in common with one another than you previously thought and using that commonality to work together for greatness.
WAYS TO CULTIVATE INTERSECTIONALITY	• ·Learn Maslow Hierarchy of Needs • ·Coat of Arms Activity • ·Hopefulness Survey by Dr. Karen Boyd • ·Diversity Dimensions Wheel Chart • ·Iceberg Chart • ·What's in a Name Activity

In summary, as a superhero, Dr. Boyd brings insightfulness to the table and advanced understanding of intersectionality. What will you bring to the table to advance intersectionality in programs and services in the workplace? What cape will you wear when you develop insightful programs and services for intersectionality? In the final chapter, the author will share additional resources and the survey of Hopefulness created by Dr. Boyd to assist leaders and organizations with cultivating bold intersectionality for greatness.

1. Organizations should leverage intersectionality as a new way to enhance their diversity and inclusion programs and services in the workplace.

2. Without leveraging intersectionality in programs and services, organizations will continue to be impacted by low productivity, satisfaction and engagement, and high attrition with diverse employees.

3. Intersectionality is connected to sense of belonging and mattering.

4. Embracing the way we intersect with one another can facilitate how we can discover more common ground.

BIG INTERACTIONS

"Diverse interactions is connecting with others to witness and support their journey. Bringing together all walks of life professionals and the community to make positive generational change."

— **Dr. Michelle Robin**

Leveraging Diverse Interactions

The second BIG "I" the author believes that individuals and organizations need to leverage for effective employee engagement is ensuring there are multicultural and diverse interactions. Interactions are a kind of action that occurs as two or more objects influence one another. The idea of a two-way effect is essential in the concept of interactions, as opposed to a one-way causal effect. Far too often, you still witness employees working and socializing in monocultural groups. The opposite of interactions is working in isolation or silos and the absence of trust. Engaging this way limits our ability to have meaningful relationships and fulfilled lives. Multicultural interactions is all about leveraging highly engaged situations that

Great efforts of diversity will help all people appreciate the similarities, differences, nuances, and cultural pillars to create better products, make less-subjective decisions in hiring, think "who's not at the table but should be" and produce better leaders."

— **Laura Isabel Alvarez**

position employees for the opportunity to encounter diverse interactions, diverse networks, and diverse connections for success. Over time, leveraging big diverse interactions in programs and services between employees, groups, and teams is key toward building trust, respect, and appreciation for effective, ongoing diverse relationships. In order to leverage big interactions, organizations must incorporate this approach throughout their programs and services, such as being intentional about creating diverse interactions from the attraction, recruitment, development, and succession- planning life stages in the workplace. "The far-bigger issue is how people interact with each other once they're on the job," says Howard J. Ross, founder and chief learning officer at the diversity consultancy Cook Ross. He cites an often-quoted maxim: "Diversity is being invited to the party; inclusion is being asked to dance, and a sense of belonging is being able to choose the music."

Experiencing Diverse Interactions

As organizations move from leveraging big interactions to experiencing big interactions, they must ensure that the six-diversity national best practices are incorporated for intentional interactions and engagement to occur around diversity and inclusion. The six national diversity best practices the author experiences throughout her work and suggests others do the same to lead in a big way are: the law of the land, changing demographics, the buying power, safe and productive environments, the smart/right thing to do, and the business case for diversity and inclusion. Oftentimes, many leaders hold true to only one basic practice as a guide to what drives their engagement programs and services in the workplace around diversity and inclusion — that is the law of the land.

But experiencing diverse interactions is not based solely on what the law requires. It is about authentic diverse connections and networks that are built with others for success and how well those connections lead to personal and professional growth. Interactions and connections are important in everything we do in life. Creating diverse interactions in the workplace will shape diversity character and challenge our social consciousness — helping us to land on the proactive side in our efforts internally and externally throughout our organizations and society as a whole.

And that is just one half of the equation — let's talk about the buying power or economic side of the equation that is absolutely critical for the success of this work. If

> *The more connected you are, the more visible you are.*
>
> **— Debbie Bass**
> **Vice President**

organizations are not focused on diversity greatness that capitalizes on harnessing the buying power of diverse populations, then organizations are going to lose in the long run. Leaders must work and continue to embrace best practices, changing demographics, and the other critical areas that underscore diversity best practices to ensure that the boldness of their approaches results in the greater good for all. We are rapidly becoming a more ethnically and multi-culturally diverse country day by day; by 2020, this will compel leaders of our country to make great strides toward more diverse interactions.

Bold interactions focus on how those innumerable diverse interactions, networks, and connections lead to greatness throughout our lives. Multiple diverse interactions in the workplace play a key role in shaping an employee's success. From the very beginning of our existence, our interactions with family, friends, and those who influence our lives, as well as those we influence help to define our perception of great interaction. It also influences our ability to boldly interrelate with those around us based on how relative the act is to our desired outcome, whether it be in our community or in our workplace. If leaders keep these six best practices in mind as they develop and design engagement programs and services, organizations will be able to deliver on their promises more often than not. Through many diverse-employee-engagement experiences in the workplace, they learn what they should do (or not do) with others, they learn how to adjust their interactions given the situation, and they learn who they should (and should not) interact with to create a desired outcome.

We are continually developing our intended purpose for specific interactions, whether it is to further our relationships or build personal networks for our targeted goals and objectives. There is a great saying that the author believes still rings true today: "It is not necessarily what you know but who you know that leverages big interactions in life and at work." For example, 80-85% of career opportunities or opportunities in general are usually based on that exact saying. Let's review some research that further defines the impact of this idea for diverse employees.

Diversity in the American workplace was virtually nonexistent for the first 150 years after the country's founding. World War I, the 1920s Jazz Age, and a stronger voice among minority workers slowly changed the workplace from a white-male domain to better reflect a multicultural society. Still, the passage of federal laws and the formation of activist groups have not guaranteed racial and gender equality in the workplace.

When we interact with others, it is typically in response to a need, or it is an act with the sole purpose of inspiring actions designed to meet one's need. In either case, interacting is an element meant to meet what one perceives as a need. President Harry Truman integrated the U.S. military in 1948, sparking mass change in the workplace. President John Kennedy, in 1961, established the Commission on the Status of Women to improve hiring practices and maternity leave. The Equal Pay Act followed in 1963, making it illegal to pay women less than a man working in the same position. The 1964 Civil Rights Act was signed by President Lyndon Johnson. In each case, the response to a "perceived need" led to an interactive act or movement that ignited change in society. In today's business environment, diversity is a perceived need. Unfortunately, organizations tend to address this issue in response to the need. More effort is placed on attracting a diverse applicant pool, rather than creating an environment that attracts diverse talent capable of thriving within an environment ready to embrace the whole person, not only the skill. Because most organizations seek only to respond to the need for diversity, the success of their accomplishments is short-lived, due to the diverse talent placed in an environment where low diverse interaction opportunities are created for success. The diverse employee feels restricted or underappreciated in the workplace.

Developing Diverse Interactions

In some cases, we've lost the ability to have great relationships, big interactions, or big connections in organizations not because it's what we should want but just because of the way things are. We operate with lack of knowledge, with limited understanding; we've become more diverse and less connected with our own social norms or discrete ethnic and cultural upbringings. Organizations have not come full circle on how to develop or incorporate successful diverse interactions in programs and services. It has become difficult for some organizations to facilitate diverse interactions because of the mobility of many roles now. If done right, the mobility of roles can cause some employees to increase their interactions and connections with people who are different — and not see these opportunities as fearful. It will take big steps to get to meaningful interactions, more big steps to get to intentional inclusion, and even more big steps to get to big, bold outcomes for greatness.

There are three resources that the author has found useful on her journey: The Tolerance Scale, the On Common Ground activity, and the Leadership Network Diagnostic (LND) tool. The Tolerance Scale is a great learning tool — a highly effective scale to help individuals explore how biases and assumptions impact interactions and decisions in the workplace. The scale helps you understand better that our attitudes toward differences come from our life experiences, early messages, and core values and beliefs. In most cases, they are hard to change. During this process, individuals increase their knowledge about the differences that impact behaviors. Differences don't have to be about primary dimension of diversity, such as race, gender, ethnicity, or age. They can be about any dimension such as work style, generational differences, language, education, or even the way someone dresses. Each of these areas pose challenges for interactions in the workplace. The On Common Ground activity allows for individuals to explore and to develop effective interactions that create awareness about the differences and commonalities present within the group or team. This activity concludes with individuals walking away with a better awareness of common connections. Finally, the author experienced the Leadership Network Diagnostic (LND) tool while attending a women's leadership program. The creator of the Leader Network Diagnostic, Phil Willburn designed the tool to map the communication networks of effective leaders and to help leaders and senior teams in organizations create more effective interactions and networks. It is a very powerful diagnostic to help individuals sharpen their ability to cultivate the right types of networks for effective interactions.

Interaction is not only an active ingredient within the conversation of diversity but as a necessity that began with diverse interaction studies in the late 1990s. Researchers like Dr. Patricia Gurin argued that structural diversity is a necessary precursor for diverse interactions to occur. She stated that, "Diverse ideas and information have entered the academy largely due to the presence and efforts of diverse people (Gurin, 1999)." Gruin explained that it is impossible to interact with diverse people if they are not represented within the environment. For far too long, businesses were attempting to address the issue of diversity without actually interacting with those the discussion involved. By walking in others' shoes is another great approach to having greater appreciation for others and facilitating more inclusive programs and services. Let's take a look at two super-shero stories from Dr. Michelle Robin and Laura Alvarez of how they championed interactions by leveraging, experiencing, developing, and cultivating diverse interactions throughout their work.

Dr. Michelle Robin, who has been around wellness for nearly three decades, is an international speaker, best-selling author, and practicing chiropractor. She is the founder of Your Wellness Connection, P.A., one of the nation's most successful integrative healing centers focusing on disciplines such as chiropractic, Chinese medicine, massage therapy, energy medicine, counseling, nutritional and wellness coaching, and movement arts. She is an accomplished author of numerous books focused on integrated health strategies promoting well-being. Dr. Robin also consults with businesses, non-profits, and faith-based communities in developing wellness programs. She has spoken on improving individual well-being as well as developing a culture of wellness, to a wide variety of groups and organizations throughout the United States.

The Masters Circle nationally recognized Dr. Robin as 2007 Chiropractor of the Year. Most recently, Dr. Robin has been a key member to many wellness-and-business-focused organizations in Kansas City, as well as received many honors and awards for her efforts in business and the community.

BIG: Interactions Story

Dr. Michelle Robin is a Chief Wellness Officer of Your Wellness Connection, P.A. She has been leveraging diverse interactions in her life and work for more than 30 years helping hundreds of thousands of individuals in the U.S. and globally. Based on her big impact throughout Kansas City, Michelle displays amazing ability to interact with diverse individuals on all level. She displays the "epic" super-shero characteristic of diversity and inclusion. "Epic" is about the person who has a series of extraordinary achievements or events that is elevated to a high level by an extraordinary individual. She has brought new insight to the field by applying diversity and inclusion principles to personal health. The dictionary defines wellness as a "dynamic state of health in which an individual progresses toward a higher level of functioning, achieving an optimum balance between internal and external environments." Because of a deep understanding of the application of this definition, Dr. Robin has taken her vision of health well beyond merely the absence of disease. Her approach to health is based on the concept of achieving a higher level of functioning in partnership with clients. She leverages diverse interactions with those partnerships on a regular basis. Dr. Robin states, "In order to achieve wellness, you must address and proactively care for the whole person. By using a wellness model, which incorporates natural, complementary disciplines and includes a participative approach to health, individuals are empowered to make wellness choices and achieve balance in all areas of health."

Dr. Robin's life-changing passion with chiropractic care began at the age of 15, when she was injured playing sports. She received chiropractic care from Dr. John Lakin, and, to her amazement, she recovered quickly from the injury and felt relief from chronic sinusitis and sore throats. Dr. Robin credits Dr. Lakin's and his wife, Carol's, holistic approach to health using acupuncture, energy medicine, and philosophy that health is more than the body's physical aspects. Further, they gave her direction on her spiritual path, teaching her she had unlimited potential to become anything she dreamed of being. This proved to be instrumental during a later journey of recovery and discovery, when, at age 31, she experienced a serious meltdown and had to do some deep work and unpack the impact of societal programming concerning both gender preferences and sexual orientation. Dr. Robin states, "I learned to rely on the wisdom of the Holy Spirit and the magic of people being placed in your life for a reason." She learned the importance of pausing and being in the moment and began taking up the mantel of "rebooting" up-and-coming generations through her work with diverse populations, thus leveraging diverse interactions through these life experiences.

As Dr. Robin witnessed personal-health transformations through this inclusive healing system, she was led to adopt an underutilized model as she worked alongside Richard Yennie, Chiropractor and Diplomate in Acupuncture, while in chiropractic school. Acclaimed as bringing acupuncture to the United States, Dr. Yennie played a pivotal role in Dr. Robin's quest to transform people's lives through healing. Dr. Yennie introduced her to four aspects of healing based on eastern philosophy: mechanical, chemical, energetic, and psychological/spiritual. Dr. Michelle Robin attributes the Lakins' mentorship, Dr. Richard Yennie's wisdom, and the leadership of other healing teachers to have positively influenced her life's mission — to heal, love, and educate herself and others with integrity, humor, and spirit.

Dr. Robin's pursuit of her mission led her to create a remarkable tool — The 4 Quadrants to Wellbeing — as a pathway and model to understand the interactions of the critical components of health and ultimately understand the human body's profound capacity for healing when given the proper care. Here are the components and definitions that make up the model:

1. Mechanical: The physical body is influenced by how and how often you move. Extended periods of pain are harmful to your body performing optimally. By the time you feel pain and discomfort, you have likely had an issue for quite some time. Pain is your body's way of getting your attention.

2. Chemical: The body's chemistry is influenced by what enters it and what is released in its effort to maintain a state of balance, called homeostasis. You are what you consume and what your body absorbs from the environment. The body is masterful with detoxifying systems if they are adequately supported.

3. Energetic: The life-energy that courses through your body is influenced by external environments and energy sources. Healing can be accomplished by shifting energy to correct imbalances in the body's own energy fields.

4. Psycho-Spiritual: The interconnections between the mind and spirit influence the body in ways that are undeniable and not fully understood. Emotional and spiritual blocks can stress the body, creating pain and dysfunction.

According to Dr. Robin, "You can make small changes that result in big shifts in your health and well-being and put the odds in your favor of living a fulfilling and thriving life." True wellness is a blending of mind-body-spirit, a journey that creates a holistic state of being that is uniquely you. This mindset is significant to the body of diversity and inclusion work in that when you feel that you are separate from others, you cannot lead a full, connected life. Conversely, one can extend their health and well-being beyond themselves to build healthy relationships, health communities, and ultimately a health society through diverse interactions. Realizing that life is a combination of simple things that impact your life helps to form healthy, lifelong habits that promote the good of the individual as well as the good of all. According to Dr. Robin, "Great diversity efforts, it is getting the medical community to be inclusive of all providers for the best interest of our consumers." This BIG book on diversity and inclusion provides us with a tool to help navigate the pivotal point in humanity that we are confronting today.

BIG: Interactions Story

Laura Alvarez is an innovative, dedicated business growth leader. She has spent the past 10 years honing her positive, motivated, supportive, and approachable work process to develop multi-functional teams across a wide variety of industry settings, including union, nonprofit, and corporate environments. She has spent her professional life leveraging relationships to build and execute programs with both English- and Spanish-speaking populations. She is a member of a leading Latino professional organization and has served in impactful leadership roles in major financial and not-for-profit organizations.

Laura Isabel Alvarez is an innovative program executive and consultant who has worked in both for-profit and nonprofit organizations. She has been leveraging diverse interactions in her work and social life for a long time. She is known as a great social butterfly. She interacts with a broad diverse spectrum of individuals to make a difference daily. Her lifelong focus and passion is building a great community that she can be proud to develop and cultivate over time. This passion is reflected in her service on boards focused on literacy and education as well as those that are internationally culturally relevant. She also is focused on women empowerment and leadership issues. She has been on the ground floor in developing and executing growth strategies to increase the Hispanic consumer base through focused pilot programs with effective marketing and field-execution initiatives. These big outcomes were based on the power of facilitating great interactions — working cross-functionally with market-insight teams, call centers, product development, and marketing channels to create and execute campaigns.

Based on her big impact throughout Kansas City, Laura displays the "epic" super-shero characteristic of diversity and inclusion. "Epic" is about the person who has a series of extraordinary achievements or events elevated to a high level — an extraordinary individual who makes extraordinary contributions. She consistently and creatively goes "the extra mile" to seek out and embrace the opinions, feelings, and behaviors of diverse populations to ensure that communications and development of products and services result in culturally relevant market positioning. Laura states, "Effective decision making is at the heart of diversity with respect to ensuring a true reflection of the population to be served. I pay particular attention to the diverse status of individuals when building teams or focus groups to interact to ensure that a broad set of impacts are considered during planning and decision-making processes."

Laura's life-changing landmark experiences that built her diversity-interactions muscle date back to her childhood in Texas. Early on, as the eldest child in a divorced household, she assumed the roles of negotiator and intermediary for her mother who used English as a Second Language for daily-living activities such as grocery shopping and bill paying. Later as Laura began to navigate her professional career, she observed how an assistant superintendent in a major school district would intentionally seek out a cross-section of parents based on their status in addition to gender and race to elicit parental feedback on ideas and/or concerns before proceeding with recommendations or changes. Subsequent educational and professional environments, including moving to Kansas City to attend college, attending law school in South Dakota as well as her role as a community organizer strengthened her diverse interaction skills. Laura recalls a time when she used her law degree to represent the Service Employees International Union membership — a predominantly African-American janitorial and maintenance staff — who questioned her ability to fairly represent their grievances and concerns. During a meeting, she boldly stood up and asked for a time out to clear the air about the friction about not being able to represent them. At the moment, she learned an important lesson about how to grant grace to one another in order to gain greater insight and understanding.

On her journey, in addition to being direct — after all, she is from Texas! — Laura has continually utilized the IRAC Methodology from her Law School training as a best practice in building and navigating big interactions. The IRAC method is the standard of legal writing, structured to communicate logical reasoning in a precise fashion. The acronym and key components consist of the following:

I: Identify the issue

R: Rules — understand the underlying factors that apply to the situation, e.g., policies, societal norms, cultural nuances

A: Analysis — facilitate dialogue across the populations impacted

C: Conclusion — listen and formulate strategies that ensure those present gain insights and understanding, and/or figure out how to re-direct.

MEASURABLE EXPECTATIONS from the utilization of the IRAC process in diversity and inclusion setting include:

- Becoming VULNERABLE with one another
- Establishing MUTUAL LEARNING and MUTUAL EXPECTATIONS upfront
- Granting each other the GRACE OF TIME to see one another; learn from one another.

According to Laura, "You will know you are there by what people are saying about you when you are not in the room. It is easy to want to be one of the bunch. I constantly find ways to interact with people with whom I am not one of the bunch. I believe that being intentional in how I interact with others and seeking to understand who others are helps me become an effective advocator." Ultimately Laura plants seeds for those who may not be at the table or had not considered a certain perspective or point of view. " Great diversity efforts will help all people appreciate the similarities, differences, nuances, and cultural pillars to create better products, make less subjective decisions in hiring, think "who's not at the table" that should be" and produce better leaders. The BIG book provides a tool that will enable practitioners to develop, at a minimum, a baseline of understanding of diversity and inclusion and, at best, compel us as a country to move toward true inclusivity. "Now is the right time!" This book can not only impact the direction of our country; the big hope is that this BIG book will

- Help peers understand the field
- Provide "nuggets" that advance observations and actions faster
- Result in better employee-engagement decisions
- Move the diversity and inclusion field forward in a big, sustainable way

INTERACTIONS

DEFINITION OF INTERACTIONS	Connections between diverse individuals, groups and teams to build effective outcomes. Key to building trust, respect, and appreciation for effective, ongoing success.
POLAR OPPOSITE OF INTERACTIONS	The opposite of interactions is isolation/silos and an absence of trust, which limits your ability to have meaningful relationships and fulfilled lives. Limits in your ability to have meaningful relationships and fulfilled lives.
LEVERAGE INTERACTIONS	Leverage diverse interactions through a two-way effect or team effect.
EXERIENCE INERACTIONS	Experience diverse interactions by being vulnerable enough to trust and operate with an intellectual restlessness that opens you up to interact on views that support or do not support your current thinking.
DEVELOP INTERACTIONS	Develop your diverse interactions muscle by connecting with others who are culturally and ethnically different from you.
WAYS TO CULTIVATE INTERACTIONS	<ul><li>On Common Ground Activity</li><li>Leadership Network Diagnostic Tool</li><li>Personal Board of Directors Activity</li><li>TMAY Icebreaker</li><li>Tolerance Scale</li><li>Four Quadrants of Wellbeing by Dr. Michelle Robin</li></ul>

In summary, as superheroes, Dr. Michelle Robin and Laura Alvarez bring epic, advanced understanding of the importance of diverse interactions. What will you bring to the table to advance diverse interactions in the workplace? What cape will you wear when you develop epic programs and services for diverse interactions? In the final chapter, the author will share additional resources that can cultivate Bold Interactions for Greatness.

1. Organizations should leverage effective multicultural, diverse interactions for enhanced diversity and inclusion programs and services in the workplace.

2. Leveraging big interactions in programs and services between employees, groups, and teams is key toward building trust, respect, and appreciation for effective ongoing diverse relationships.

3. As organizations move from leveraging big interactions to experiencing big interactions, they must ensure that the six-diversity national best practices are incorporated for intentional interactions and engagement to occur around diversity and inclusion.

4. The six national diversity best practices that organizations should leverage and experience are: the law of the land, changing demographics, the buying power, safe and productive environments, the smart/right thing to do, and the business case for diversity and inclusion.

BIG INCLUSION

"Inclusion is the strategy requiring that all individuals be valued in both their differences and input. A variety of individuals working harmoniously and successfully towards a common goal that leads to greatness."

— **Dr. Emmanuel Ngomsi**

Leveraging Inclusion

The third BIG "I" the author believes is important to leverage as individuals and organizations is inclusion. Inclusion is different than diversity. Inclusion means that all employees have the opportunity to have full engagement in the workplace. They have a seat at the table and are leveraged for the unique perspectives they bring to the table. In order to leverage BIG in the workplace, it will require leaders to ensure that there are engaging inclusive programs and services that support a sense of belonging, a person feeling valued and safe, and that all *matter* in the workplace. If leveraged correctly, over time, the inclusive programs and services that are enhanced will allow employees to make big investments in the workplace. Inclusion is a mindset. The opposite of inclusion is exclusion and, if not leveraged correctly, exclusive practices will make more subtractions or withdrawals than deposits in employees' overall engagement in the workplace. This is a powerful concept related to the "emotional bank account" discussed by one of Stephen Covey's training principles. Over time, this will lead to helplessness, stress, low morale, and employees quitting their jobs at a higher rate. When placed within the spectrum of diversity, Bold Inclusion for Greatness occurs when people deliberately

> *Honoring and accepting others.*
>
> **— Dr. Michelle Robin**
> **Chief Wellness Officer**

extend themselves beyond the expected boundaries of race, age, gender, different interests and include others who are different from them. The advancement of the technology, entertainment industry, and the internet has facilitated our ability to reach beyond our own communities and see others who are different from us right from home. Today, we can even include other countries, and, given time, we may even tap into other universes. The possibilities are endless.

Experiencing Inclusion

The experience of exclusion is often the big push that leads to the boldness of inclusion. In general, people don't make an effort to include others unless they need something or have been the victim of exclusion themselves. It is often the experience of feeling left out, unappreciated, or even ignored that creates a calculated effort to ensure no one else has that experience. Unfortunately, we tend to believe that we have reached the end of the spectrum once we establish and cultivate an inclusion mindset for others. In reality, we have only moved to a place of ineptness. As we include others, we tend to develop a measuring stick of who and/or what is appropriate and worthy of being included within our circles. John Howard Griffin, the author of *Black Like Me*, wrote, "Humanity does not differ in any profound way; there are not essentially different species of human beings. If we could only put ourselves in the shoes of others to see how we would react, then we might become aware of the injustice of discrimination and the tragic inhumanity of every kind of prejudice." Walking in others' shoes is a great approach to having greater appreciation for others.

Bold Inclusion for Greatness suggests that organizations need to continue to develop and enhance diverse-employee-engagement programs and services with an inclusive mindset. It's no coincidence that employers with vibrant diversity and inclusion initiatives usually have highly engaged workforces. "Inclusion is a key factor in boosting employee satisfaction and performance," according to Dr. Shirley Davis, who was the vice president of global diversity and inclusion and workforce strategies at the Society for Human Resource Management (SHRM) in 2012 and now is the CEO of SDS Global Enterprises, Inc. According to her, during a SHRM webinar in 2012 titled "Inclusion Supercharges Employee Satisfaction and Performance," she stated, "You can have diversity but not inclusion in your organization." "Inclusion is the ability to engage diversity in your workforce, so that everyone has equal opportunities to contribute." "A person feels included and validated by their ability to consistently have an authentic seat at the decision-making tables within the organization."

All of us know what exclusion feels like, so individuals should take a "pulse check" with each interaction and answer the question on a conscious and sub-conscious level to determine if he/she feels included and validated within the organizational fabric with respect to engagement programs, services, and initiatives. In an article titled "Inclusive Workplaces Lead to Engaged Employees," the 2009 research from Hewitt Associates revealed that businesses with high levels of engagement and inclusion tended to have higher stock prices and stronger returns on investment for corporate shareholders. A report from Watson Wyatt (2009) found that businesses with high employee engagement and inclusion had higher productivity, lower turnover, and stronger customer loyalty.

When Affirmative Action was implemented in the early 1960s, it became apparent that diversity meant a lot more than a facelift. The addition of women, racial presence, and obvious cultural variations did little to fully embrace the concept of diversity. Court case after court case were constant reminders that, while the action of hiring an individual applied to the intent of Affirmative Action, the lack of participation and inclusion often nullified the progress desired by the government or the business. While progressive companies like Ford played a vital role in company diversity, inclusion was seldom concurrent with the term. In January 1916, Ford went from 50 black employees to 2,500 in 1920 and increased to 5,000 in 1923. In 1967, Henry Ford II said, "Opportunity is not equal when people who would make good employees are not hired because they lack the self-confidence to apply, or because the formal hiring criteria screen out potential good employees as well as potentially poor ones." Today, Ford Company proudly boasts, "Our diversity makes us a better company, a stronger company, by bringing in fresh ideas, perspectives, experiences, and life responsibilities, and by fostering a truly collaborative workplace." As a result, generations of motor-vehicle purchasers have translated diversity and inclusion into loyalty and purchasing power.

> *Inclusion means going beyond diversity to make sure that everyone is comfortable to share their own ideas.*
>
> **— Connie Russell**
> **President**

Simma Lieberman, an inclusion expert and author of *110 Ways to Champion Diversity and Inclusion*, stated, "In an inclusion culture, everyone has the opportunity to do their best work no matter who they are, what they do, or where they work." She further states that everyone feels like they're really a part of the organization, and they know they contribute to the organization's success.

It is the revelation and experiences like those of author John Howard Griffin that often move people beyond the point of being a witness of inclusion to becoming an actual participant. Participation requires one only to take part in a cause, whereas boldness in this area often requires sacrifice. Sacrifice, in and of itself, elevates one's efforts far beyond participation — it becomes the apparition of greatness, which very few are willing to become. The importance of facilitating true inclusion in terms of being able to share ideas, provide input regarding decision-making, and having a voice at all levels cannot be overstated.

The goal of the Civil Rights Movement was to establish rights to equal access and opportunities for the basic privileges outlined in the U.S. Constitution for *all* citizens without regard to race, gender, nationality, sexual preference, as well as one's physical or mental ability. It was the boldness of those African Americans experiencing the greatest extent of exclusion that moved this cause to international exhibitions. Once exposed, the many forms of unjust exclusionary practices that had plagued our country for centuries had to be formally addressed and disposed of in their current form. In the case of the cause for equal rights and equal pay, many individuals found themselves caught within a multi-faceted spectrum of exclusion versus inclusion. For those who were a part of the majority, White America, the question was merely, "Is this my concern?" For the employed, well-endowed African American, the question was not necessarily whether or not they were excluded, but rather to what extent. This is what the definition of ineptness looks like. In many cases, everyone else is left to define what inclusion meant for them individually and what steps are necessary to move themselves from where they were to where they wanted to be.

Anna Beninger, senior director of research and corporate engagement partner at Catalyst, conducted research (2014) that shows that an organization's formal efforts to promote inclusion may be effective, but if there is a disconnect with the informal culture, exclusion can persist. In an article, "How to Intentionally Create More Inclusive

Culture" she says, "Diversity is a fact; inclusion is a choice." "You must have a diverse workforce in order to be inclusive. When individuals feel that they belong to the group and are valued for their unique perspective and skills, they are more cooperative and innovative."

When placed within the spectrum of diversity, inclusion is the deliberate act of extending one's self beyond clear, existent boundaries. Remember, experience ignites vision. The experience of being excluded develops a boldness to include others, regardless of their differences. The Civil Rights Movement experienced its greatest success when people of all races were willing to include themselves in the cause for justice. Personal experiences tend to drive one's evaluation of aptness relative to the need for inclusion. When the motive for inclusion is selfish, the result often lacks relationship and connectivity. However, when the motive for inclusion is to cultivate a vision that incorporates diversity because of the represented differences, a unique relationship is created. Unity, inclusion, justice, and acceptance became the face of the Civil Rights Movement, not color or race. The fact is that, once we begin to boldly interact with individuals outside of our designated circle of inclusion, diversity instantly becomes a by-product. Inclusion often brings about diversity.

Developing Inclusion

The term "diversity" tends to capture an all-embracing societal ideology that seldom moves beyond the tangible race and gender. However, when inclusion is added as a key element of diversity, it broadens the introspection ideas. The conscious development of inclusion not only expands the perception of the norm but often reshapes the societal ideology that once took precedence. The author finds the Harvard Implicit Association Test (IAT) as another great resource for individuals to test their level of biases and inclusive behavior toward situations. IAT measures attitudes and beliefs that people may be unwilling or unable to share. The IAT may be especially interesting if it shows that you have an implicit attitude that you did not know about.

Erik Larson, contributing *Forbes* writer, in an article titled "Diversity and Inclusion Equals Better Decision Making At Work," conducted research using Cloverpop's data on inclusion with 200 different business teams in a wide variety of companies over two years. The research suggests that employees who build diverse and inclusive teams see the best outcomes. According to the research, teams outperform individual decision-making 66% of the time, and decision-making improves as team diversity increases. All-male teams make better business decisions 58% of the time, while gender-diverse teams do so 73% of the time. Teams that also include a wide range of ages and different geographic locations make better business decisions 87% of the time. 83% of Millennials are more actively engaged when they believe their company fosters an inclusive culture — and in 10 years, Millennials will comprise nearly 75% of the workforce. (Deloitte).

> *Inclusion is Belonging. Simple as that.*
>
> **— Carol Taylor**
> **President**

Let's look at a superhero story of Dr. Emmanuel Ngomsi, a major diversity champion who is the President of All World Languages and Cultures, Inc. He leverages, experiences, develops, and cultivates inclusion in his work in the U.S. and abroad. He is an experienced, award-winning educator, speaker, and corporate trainer. Dr. Emmanuel Ngomsi has been a champion and leading authority on diversity and inclusion subjects and practices for more than 30 years. He is a native of Cameroon and is devoted to teaching Americans about the cultures of West Africa, and to promoting a love of cultures, respect for diversity, and international experience among U.S. citizens. Dr. Ngomsi is the 1995 recipient of the National Foreign Language Fellowship Award, from the National Endowment for the Humanities and the Geraldine R. Dodge Foundation. This distinction allowed him to pursue research on teaching and learning games around the world. He is active in numerous cultural, foreign languages, educational, and professional-training associations, and has been a guest speaker, lecturer, and presenter at various national and international conferences. Dr. Ngomsi was honored as the recipient of the Missouri Municipal League Civic Leadership Award and was selected as Outstanding Citizen of the Year 2011 from a city in Missouri. Created in 1999, All World Languages and Cultures, Inc. (AWLC), located in the Kansas City, Missouri, area, is a minority-owned, certified small business offering services in the fields of diversity training, cultural education, and foreign-language service. AWLC trains and consults with corporations, government agencies, and education communities worldwide, and continues to earn special recognition from many of these corporations and agencies.

> *Inclusion is where individuals are welcomed and accepted for who they are.*
>
> **— Dr. Gerald Hannah**
> **CEO and Author**

BIG Inclusion Story

Dr. Emmanuel Ngomsi is President of all World Languages and Cultures, Inc. Dr. Ngomsi specializes in teaching about world cultures and in promoting inclusion, respect for diversity, and international experience for more than 30 years. Ngomsi spent nine years as instructor, Chief Language and Cross-Cultural Coordinator for the United States Peace Corps. He was instrumental in designing a curriculum for Peace Corps volunteers assigned to work in Francophone African countries. This experience served to spark his professional pursuit of understanding how language impacts relationships and productivity. According to Ngomsi, "When people with different cultural backgrounds or nationalities work together, there comes an inevitable moment of misunderstanding during which communication — both verbal and nonverbal — seems to hinder working relationships and productivity."

Based on his big impact on the field worldwide, Dr. Ngomsi is a "motivated and determined" superhero for diversity and inclusion. His life's work has centered on helping others understand and harness the power of language and communications to benefit personal and organizational development. His ability to apply a global perspective to specific environments enables Dr. Ngomsi to facilitate discussions across diverse workforce teams that result in more cohesive teams with a common focus that show up as big contributors to the growth of the organization regarding inclusive practices and principles.

Dr. Ngomsi's extraordinary contributions to diversity and inclusion include a 4 year development and research of Yan Koloba as a phenomenal inclusion-building tool for teams and communities in various and diverse settings. More than a million participants have experienced this powerful tool in the US, Africa, Europe, Japan, and Indonesia over the years. The origins of Yan Koloba date back to Dr. Ngomsi's African childhood. He grew up playing the game requiring 3 or more people passing blocks among themselves while singing. His early role as an educator allowed him to introduce the game to American students through funding provided by the National Endowment for the Arts. Dr. Ngomsi, in partnership with a school superintendent and school district in the south, worked with a cohort of students to prove the team-building capabilities of the game. The overwhelming positive outcomes resulted in a book titled Shocking

Cultures and a proprietary game that Dr. Ngomsi and his team utilize in all their training programs.

Yan Koloba's key principles and observable outcomes promote teamwork, understanding that everybody counts, no one is more important than another, all learning capabilities count, leverages left- and right-brain development and problem-solving skills. The impact on the individual's awareness of others is profound. Inclusiveness becomes something tangible that each person can relate to and begin to internalize with key realizations, including:

- The ability to break down barriers and BUILD TRUST

- WIN-WIN OUTCOME — EVERYONE CAN BE PRODUCTIVE

- DEVELOPS (ILLUSTRATES) THE POWER OF "1" — Individual accountability; responsibility to all; success of the team is determined by the individuals

- Through Singing — EVERY VOICE IS HEARD; no sorting; EXPERIENCE COMMONALITY

- Cognizant of the other person — you have to understand their needs; recognition of your part in the process

This is significant to the diversity field in that the game provides a vehicle through which professionals create the opportunity to "lessen cultural blunders." According to Dr. Ngomsi, "People may not know how to include new people, and, conversely, new people may not know how to fit in. It's like building a good garden — you have good seeds, and you have to have good soil that accepts and supports all the different seeds."

"Great diversity efforts is accepting, appreciating and celebrating all." according to Dr. Ngomsi. "The BIG book helps people understand inclusion and its potential regarding personal and organizational productivity. In short, this book provides a means of developing acceptance, appreciation, and celebration of a variety of dimensions. Moreover, it increases the understanding of professionals of the strategic role that all participants play — both their differences and their input should be valued."

INCLUSION

DEFINITION OF INCLUSION	The act of a person being included within a group, team or organization. Support a sense of belonging, a person feeling valued and safe, and that all matter in the workplace.
POLAR OPPOSITE OF INCLUSION	The opposite of inclusion is exclusion, where a person makes more subtractions and withdrawals with others than deposits. Lead to helplessness, stress, low morale, and employees quitting their jobs at a higher rate.
LEVERAGE INCLUSION	Leverage inclusion by being visible and having a seat and a voice at the table.
EXERIENCE INCLUSION	Experience inclusion by cultivating a mindset of active, intentional, and ongoing efforts of reciprocal collaboration efforts.
DEVELOP INCLUSION	Develop inclusion by learning from others experiences overtime and recognizing that inclusion is not a single event but an ongoing process.
WAYS TO CULTIVATE INCLUSION	<ul><li>· Harvard IAT Assessment</li><li>· Diversity Dimensions Wheel Chart</li><li>· Vision Board</li><li>· Diversity Name Game</li><li>· RESPECT Poster</li><li>· Building a House Fable/Story/Book</li></ul>

In summary, as a superhero, Dr. Ngomsi brings motivation and determination to the table in order to advance the understanding of inclusion. What will you bring to the table to advance inclusivity in the workplace? What cape will you wear when you develop motivated and determined programs and services for inclusion? In the final chapter, the author will share additional resources and the resources of Dr. Ngomsi, which can cultivate the Bold Inclusion for Greatness.

- Ensure inclusion is at the center of all programs and services. "Inclusion" is different from "diversity." "Inclusion" means that all employees can have full engagement in the workplace.
- Ensure that there are engaging inclusive programs and services that support a sense of belonging, a person feeling valued and safe, and that all matter in the workplace.
- Inclusion often brings about diversity.

 *BIG IDEAS*

> *"Diverse ideas are a result of one's experiences in the environment and through which lens that individual chooses to view the situation. It is including others to provide better balance for better outcomes."*

— **Dr. Keith Harris**

Leveraging [Diverse] Ideas

The fourth area the author believes has a huge impact on transforming individuals and organizations is the ability to leverage diverse ideas, perspectives, and thoughts of all employees. "Diverse ideas" is defined as employees bringing different cultures, backgrounds, and personalities to the table — and allowing those differences to shape how they creatively think. This approach indicates that there is more than one way to leverage greater outcomes for enhanced ideas in programs and services. A new or original idea can often lead to innovation and the possibilities of bringing new intentions in the workplace. The opposite of diverse ideas is being closed-minded, always doing the same thing, and being stuck in a rut. Over time, this will limit employees' ability to generate new and different paths to greatness out of fear of failure to engage with others. The more variety you have in experiences and understandings of different employees, the more your employees will be able to come up with diverse ideas or solutions that defy being stuck in a rut. Over time, if one leverages the best outcomes of others' diverse ideas, then the value of others' opinions can be free from bias or limiting filters. The person has the openness to leverage and see other viewpoints and to be okay with that. Bold Ideas for Greatness is cultivated by the understanding that a diverse environment incorporates diverse ideas. Diverse ideas come from diverse experiences; diverse experiences come from a diverse workforce.

Experiencing Diverse Ideas

In the early stages of our lives, we often used our imaginations to create boxcars and clubhouses from cardboard boxes and exotic adventures by navigating trees and bushes through a park or our own backyards.

> *Not only thinking outside the box – taking the box and throwing it away!*
>
> **— Kelli Wilkins**
> **HR Leader**

It often began with, "Hey, I have an idea!" It wasn't until we got older and our peers began to dismiss our ideas as childish and lacking the commonality of the world around us. Our ideas soon became insignificant because they were considered small and unworthy of mass consideration. Much like those adventures we idealized as children, most organizations' ideas should serve the purpose of creating experiences for "everyone" on the team to enjoy.

In February 2008, Peter W. Hom collaborated on a research paper titled "Challenging Conventional Wisdom About Who Quits: Revelations from Corporate America." This research served as a validation to the concerns some companies expressed about how corporate America was struggling to retain women and minority employees. While never really answering the question "Why?" the research ignited a conversation that gave way to the notion that inclusive conversation is essential to the diversity of an organization. Hom concluded that corporations might not fully diversify until they diligently sought ways to retain diverse employees among their ranks and leverage their ideas and perspectives.

> *Be intellectually restless – that is, open to interact on views that either support or not support my current thinking.*
>
> **— Greg Valdovino**
> **Director of Diversity**

Susan Woods, author of *Thinking About Diversity of Thought*, explains, "Diversity of thought — the idea of more-than-one-way — is key to understanding the potential of diversity and inclusion as an organizational resource. The way each of us interprets and negotiates the world around us is informed by our identity, culture, and experience. Greater diversity means greater variation in perspectives and approaches." She suggests that there are three factors organizational leadership must consider in order to access and leverage diversity of thought: "the willingness, the readiness, and the opportunity." By mixing up the types of thinkers in the workplace, Deloitte believes companies can stimulate creativity, spur insight, and increase efficiency. Varying the types of thinkers in a company also helps guard against "groupthink." Diversity of thought, or "thought diversity" is still an emerging field. — "Why 'Thought Diversity' Is the Future of the Workplace,' Alison Griswold.

Developing Diverse Ideas

Study after study has shown that diversity leads to more creative teams and increases a company's bottom line. According to McKinsey, companies ranking in the top quartile of executive-board diversity were 35% likelier to financially outperform the industry medians. One of Hendrick's favorite books is *Thought Revolution: How to Unlock Your Inner Genius,* by William Donius. She met Donius more than 8 years ago at a conference where he was the keynote speaker on his novel approach to leveraging and cultivating diverse ideas and thinking. The "thought-revolution" concept spoke to her heart. The book is about when individuals live in a world where it's easy to stay stuck in ingrained patterns and behaviors. Learning to tap into the right hemisphere of the brain is the literal way to think differently about the obstacles, barriers, and even lies people tell themselves. *Thought Revolution* invites readers to unlock their whole brain to change the way they see themselves and find the

> *When one person in the group views themselves as insignificant, then they make the assumption that their diverse ideas and perspectives are not welcomed.*
> *So, they leave – taking their sometimes amazing diverse ideas with them.*
>
> **— Dr. Andrea Hendricks**
> **Author**

truth in whatever challenges them. Encompassing twelve years of research, the author of the "Thought Revolution" book took the attendees of the conference on an unexpected journey that set them free from their conventional thinking to a revolutionary approach that made lasting life changes. The book offers thought-provoking yet easy-to-do exercises, help readers to connect more fully with the needs of their subconscious right brains and unlock their hidden genius.

Let's look at a superhero story of how one diversity champion leverages, experiences, develops, and cultivates diverse ideas and perspectives throughout his work. Dr. Keith Harris is a faculty member at Kansas State University in Manhattan, Kansas, who has focused his life's work of more than 30 years on unlocking the power of diversity of knowledge to understand and solve some of

> *Diverse ideas/perspectives are ideas that challenge black and white; they think in color.*
>
> **— Kelli Wilkins**
> **HR Leader**

> *Providing platforms for others to learn about and experience diversity.*
>
> **— Debbie Bass**
> **Vice President**

the world's problems. Dr. Harris contends that many of the solutions rest with undiscovered knowledge that is dispersed geographically and culturally. "We seek to add to the knowledge base that can overcome issues and problems." He serves as an Assistant Professor of Agricultural Economics at Kansas State and a Visiting Professor at a major university in Kansas City, Missouri. Dr. Harris emphasizes teaching pedagogy that demonstrates the real-life context of problem solving. His problem-solving advocacy extends to his community engagement and board appointments. Prior to his joining Kansas State University, Dr. Harris worked with major food companies in the United States. Prior to a career in corporate America, he served as a Peace Corps volunteer in Honduras, where he worked in agribusiness market development for tropical agricultural crops.

BIG Ideas Story

Dr. Keith D. Harris is the Assistant Professor of Agricultural Economics and USDA National Needs Fellow at Kansas State University. Based on his big impact on an international scale, Dr. Harris exemplifies what it means to be a courageous superhero for diversity and inclusion. In the midst of a successful career in the food industry, Keith made the bold decision to leave to pursue his Doctorate at The University of Missouri-Columbia. This big move resulted in a career path that enabled Dr. Harris to evaluate his industry experience through a research lens for greater impact. This has resulted in landmark research published in peer-reviewed academic journals which focus on topics related to agribusiness management, financial and environmental sustainability, and food networks. The findings are presented at local, national and international conferences for industry and academic audiences. His research findings highlight how companies that collaborate strategically experience a market increase in competitiveness, sustain supply-chain performance, and are able to preserve their own identity and autonomy.

Keith's courageous superhero quality is further amplified by the life-changing decision to join the Peace Corps and serve in remote, underdeveloped, tropical environments after completing his undergraduate education. He entered the Peace Corps (1987-1990) at a time when there was no reference point in his family. No one in his family had ever voluntarily sought out opportunities where African Americans represented less than 1% of the population and the total multi-cultural percentage was 3%. In addition, Keith worked in Honduras, a foreign environment where food, language, and customs were very different from his. This big, courageous experience provided a valuable, lifelong lesson. He learned that he had so much more in common with the other volunteers than the people of the countries, and this provided the pivotal opportunity to break down stereotypes of African-Americans as well as kindle a spirit of being open to learning from others in their environments.

Throughout his courageous journey, Dr. Harris has principally relied on the use of academic databases as a tool to create big ideas. In his work, he sifts through academic literature across sectors and builds upon the research and findings of others to discover techniques that can be applied to the problem at hand. He is astute enough to integrate the key insights of others into practical problem-solving approaches. His research-professional process provides us with insight into how to approach a problem in the first place, mainly that:

- Historical perspective has value, and there are models that exist that can be studied and learned from.

- One's work shall be finished someday, but one's education never (Alexander Dumas 1856); there is a spark of an idea in everything we learn and encounter.

- Every place on your journey, someone is there to support you. Slow the process down so that you can take stock and really see the circumstances surrounding the issue.

- Diverse ideas are a result of one's experience in the environment and the lens through which the individual chooses to view the problem.

- It is prudent to view a problem from many perspectives to provide a balance or, at the very least, consideration of diverse stakeholders. This helps to minimize unintended consequences.

"Great diversity efforts is the freedom of the human spirit to purse its purpose in this world. It is a moral pursuit to enrich the lives of others without denigrating the existing works of others." according to Dr. Harris. "This BIG book on diversity and inclusion is important for where we are today. As a society, we still have very pressing issues, and if we continue to rely on past practices of the same groups of people, we will not be equipped to solve the problem. This book forces us to look outside those traditional sources and practices; it compels us to seek other expertise to solve the problem. We must stretch and pull from other spaces and break the habit of hoping to draw inspiration from the same well over and over again, in order to resolve issues and make bold breakthroughs."

IDEAS

DEFINITION OF IDEAS	Diverse ideas, perspectives, and thoughts for greater outcomes. See and value things in a different way. More than one way or approach to achieving goals or outcomes with others' diverse ideas or perspectives. The value of others' opinions can be free from bias or filters.
POLAR OPPOSITE OF IDEAS	The opposite of diverse ideas is more of the same, staying in a rut, or sticking with traditional practices and processes. Limits our ability to generate a new and different path to greatness.
LEVERAGE IDEAS	Leverage diverse ideas and perspectives by allowing others to bring their creativity to the workplace, because there is more than one way or approach to achieve greatness. Asking others thoughts and opinions.
EXERIENCE IDEAS	Experience diverse ideas and perspectives when you are invited to participate in projects and teams that honor your ideas and contributions.
DEVELOP IDEAS	Develop diverse ideas and perspectives by challenging the tried-and-true, the black-and-white. You learn to flourish in the gray area while thinking of the possibilities. Generate something better than one could do individually.
WAYS TO CULTIVATE IDEAS	• Thought Revolution Exercises • Vision Board Exercise Book(s) • Wisdom of the Crowds • Thought Revolution by William Donius

In summary, as a superhero, Dr. Harris brings courageousness to the table to advance the understanding of diverse ideas. What will you bring to the table to advance diverse ideas in the workplace? What cape will you wear when you develop courageous programs and services for diverse ideas? In the final chapter, the author will share additional resources that can cultivate Bold Ideas for Greatness.

- Huge impact on transforming an organization's programs and services for diverse employees is the ability to leverage diverse ideas, perspectives, and thoughts of all employees.
- Greater diversity means greater variation in perspectives and approaches.
- The best outcome of diverse ideas is the value of others' opinions and freedom from bias or filters.
- Bold Ideas for Greatness are cultivated by the understanding that a diverse environment incorporates diverse ideas. Diverse ideas come from diverse experiences; diverse experiences come from a diverse workforce.

BIG INNOVATION

"Innovation is the new that creates value. Building diverse teams to enhance and leverage our collective performance in order to innovative more"

— **Tammy Broaddus**

Leveraging Innovation

The fifth BIG "I" the author believes should be leveraged for greater impact with individuals and organizations is innovation. Innovation is all about engaging the diversity of the workforce for greater creativity and success. Innovation can be defined simply as a "new idea, device, or method." Diversity fosters a more creative and innovative workforce. Diverse employees need innovative programs and services that offer varied experiences and perspectives in order to fully leverage and contribute in the workplace. Over time, these innovative programs and services must be utilized to drive value creation, new ideas, new methods, and better solutions. The positive implications of diversity are usually acknowledged in terms of cognitive outcomes, such as greater innovation, ideas, and creativity that employees from distinct social backgrounds could bring.

The opposite of not leveraging innovative diverse programs and services in the workplace is what we have seen for many years. At this level, organizations that are doing the same thing, stuck in a rut, not willing to change, and clinging to traditional approaches to programs and services will not be able to retain diverse employees. Nothing stifles innovation faster than indifference, which lies at the other end of the spectrum of innovation as well. Indifference is the polar opposite of innovation. Over time, this will lead to dissatisfaction and low engagement. Bold Innovation for Greatness is the ability to utilize varied experiences and perspectives to drive creation. It is the aptitude to launch groundbreaking ideas from a bow entangled with concepts enriched with experience, culture, and the uniqueness that makes mankind the unbelievable work of art it is.

Experiencing Innovation

> *Diversity of thought is a advantage to innovation.*
>
> **— Connie Russell**
> **President**

Ekaterina Walter, contributing writer of "Reaping the Benefits of Diversity in Modern Business Innovation" in *Forbes Insights*, states, "Diversity is critical for an organization's ability to innovate and adapt in a fast-changing environment." To gain a better understanding of the role that diversity and inclusion play in organizations around the world, *Forbes Insight* conducted a comprehensive survey of more than 300 senior executives. The research concluded that the business case for diversity and inclusion is intrinsically linked to an organization's innovation strategy. Survey respondents overwhelmingly agreed that a diverse and inclusive workforce brings the different perspectives that an organization needs to power the innovation strategy. A person experiences innovation and diversity in the workplace by bringing together creative ideas and perspectives, with an inclusive team to do that. And it fuels, it ignites everything else. Our future is predicated upon having everyone at the table. And the greatness is being able to leverage that. "Innovation is in the secondary dimension of diversity definition, and it is powerful in action. Diversity leaders have seen fantastic results firsthand when innovation comes from diverse groups such as business resource groups

(BRGs), employee resource groups (ERGs), and cross-cultural mentoring strategies. When these strategies are employed, products are developed more rapidly, market share increases exponentially, and the productivity and satisfaction of diverse employees increases,"

Developing Innovation

One can develop effective innovation programs and services. According to a 2011 Forbes Survey, 85% of enterprises surveyed agreed that diversity resulted in the most innovative ideas. Companies found that the broader the spectrum of talent they embraced, the greater the innovation. In the field of agricultural economics, Keith D. Harris came to understand the importance of having all the key players at the table to minimize the unintended consequences of exclusion and to drive greater innovation. "We equally include the welfare of people and the environment to address problems. So, it is common for us to include a conservationist and a sociologist in our various discussions to provide a better balance or, at the very least, the consideration of key stakeholders."

In 2012, the *McKinsey Quarterly* published a piece titled "Is There Payoff from Top-Team Diversity?" The authors, Thomas Barta, Markus Kleiner, and Tilo Neumann, explained they examined the returns on equity (ROE), and margins on earnings before interest and taxes (EBIT) of 180 publicly traded companies located in France, Germany, the United Kingdom, and the United States. In conducting this research over a two-year period, they wanted to score a company's diversity by focusing on two company groups to ensure they objectively measured the data. They specifically measured women and foreign nationals on senior executive teams, using the latter as a proxy for cultural diversity. Once completed, the research showed that the EBIT margins at the most diverse companies were 14% greater, on average, than those of the least diverse companies. This would suggest that these results clearly demonstrate that innovative diversity has the ability to translate into equitable gains.

As innovation becomes more of a key differentiator for the world's largest companies, these organizations increasingly see having a diverse and inclusive workforce as critical to driving the creation and execution of new products, services, and business processes. Bringing together workers with different qualifications, backgrounds, and experiences are all key to effective problem-solving on the job. Similarly, diversity breeds creativity and innovation. Of 321 large global enterprises — companies with at least $500 million in annual revenue — surveyed in a *Forbes* study in 2011 titled "Workplace Diversity Key to Innovation," 85% agreed or strongly agreed that diversity is crucial to fostering innovation in the workplace.

Numerous resources and tools that have been created over the past 15 years related to innovation. Two resources the author recommends for individuals or organizations to check out are: "Infinium" and "Overflow" in the Greater Kansas City Area. A great resource for driving innovative efforts is Sue Mosby, Founder and CEO of Infinium, an innovation consultancy. For more than 30 years, she has helped senior leaders envision strategic direction, capture new growth opportunities, imagine new products and service lines, and build innovation competency in their organizations. Her unique ability to merge creativity and design thinking with diversity approaches enables her clients to build the mindset, skillset, toolset, and process to succeed.

Second, let's look at a superhero story of Tammy Broaddus on how she leverages, experiences, develops, and cultivates innovation in her work. She is a Principal at Overflow and specializes in strategy, marketing, organizational change, and corporate learning. Overflow helps accelerate idea adoption through story by launching strategy, propelling movements, and shifting perception. The company believes in a multidisciplinary approach to diffuse ideas and create behavior change. Using story design, multimedia production, events, and platform distribution, the Overflow subsidiaries of Story Lab, Meetings & Incentives, and Originals create impact for clients to get ideas adopted. Prior to Overflow, she operated her own consulting practice and had 20 years of cross-functional experience as an executive at a major global retail corporation. Tammy is also an adjunct professor in Entrepreneurship.

BIG Innovation Story

Tammy Broaddus is the Principal at Overflow and believes the biggest problem with innovation today is not discovery — it's adoption. Tammy has leveraged big innovation throughout her career. Based on her big impact locally and globally, Tammy can be best characterized as a daring superhero for diversity and inclusion. Storytelling is about creating human connection. The Overflow approach magnifies the human connection through story structure, organizational-change principles and diffusion of innovation theory. Overflow helps accelerate the adoption of ideas through story. Their work has assisted hundreds of corporate and nonprofit clients and the people they serve. And as first put forth in her master's thesis focused on corporate learning theory, Tammy Broaddus consistently uses bold organizational knowledge creation to impact productivity and profitability models. Additionally, Tammy seeks to understand how social practices and leadership behaviors affect employee knowledge or "true beliefs" and thus the implications for a given firm's knowledge creation and ultimately, its competitive advantage. Tammy states, "An important underpinning of employee knowledge are the cultural beliefs that preclude knowledge creation and thwart corporate learning. Such socialized practices can influence employee beliefs and thus corporate learning, including communication transparency, decision-making, and accountability."

Tammy's daring quality is further amplified by her cited life-changing leap — leaving a successful career of 20 years at a major retail organization to pursue her master's degree and eventually step into the emerging field of idea adoption. This proved to be a visionary move on her part; she successfully navigated uncharted innovation waters that led to her co-ownership of a start-up believing that the use of stories to spread ideas can also lead to diversity and inclusion across social systems. According to Broaddus, "If we want true innovation and new approaches to solve complex problems then we must see our worlds through a multi-lens, align our values, and respect diverse people and views."

Throughout her innovation journey, Tammy Broaddus has relied on a powerful technique to help individuals and organizations effectively tap into the potential of idea adoption. It is an experimental technique that social psychologists have used since the early 1980s to measure what's called Perspective Taking, popularized by Daniel Pink, recognized as one of the leading business thought leaders. It is the ability to get out of your own head and see things from someone else's point of view. Here's how it works:

- Identify your dominant hand.
- With your dominant hand, snap your fingers five times very quickly.
- With an erasable marker, draw a capital E on your forehead.
- The direction the E is written describes your natural tendency to view the world:
  - If you draw the E as you would read it (if not on your head) — from your perspective.

- If you draw the E as others read it on your forehead —
from another's perspective.

What really matters is context. According to Pink, "If you gradually lose the ability to see the world through another's eyes, all the experience and expertise you've accumulated will melt into a puddle of unrealized potential. But if you work to balance power and perspective taking, you'll become a more effective leader because you'll offer reasons beyond "I said so" for why anybody should follow you. You will avoid what could be the biggest mistake that bosses, teachers, executives, government officials, and anyone else in a position of power can make. The mistake is this: thinking you're the smartest person in the room. If you think you're the smartest person in the room, you've just proved that you're not. Believing that you're the smartest person in the room — trust me on this — never ends well. Remember the lesson of the "E Test." Argue like you're right but listen like you're wrong. Use your power but sharpen your perspective-taking."

So, what's the significance? The "E Test," according to Tammy, "helps us to understand how difficult or easy it is for us to see through someone else's lens. If that is not our natural tendency, we can learn to do it by merely asking, 'If this was me, how would I feel and what would I think?' This is the first step to getting your ideas adopted. Innovation is the new that creates value. I build teams who have shared values and high diversity in information and experience to enhance our collective performance."

We must learn and accept that innovation is often created from a diverse group of people. If we don't have diversity at the table, then we don't have multiple perspectives to foster constructive debate and elevate thought processes through "creative abrasion." This allows us to be more open to and understand what's needed for BIG experimentation to get started, learn on the fly, and adapt as ideas move forward. The approach translates to innovation and entrepreneurship by proving out concepts (on the cheap) and adapting as they move forward rather than over-engineering and over-investing in ideas before experimenting.

According to Broaddus, "Great diversity efforts can exist if people respectfully connect with others and love themselves." Only then can the trust develop that allows for compassion and empathy when times get tough. "The BIG book on diversity and inclusion is important for one simple reason: it confronts us with the reality that, if we fail to listen, we will fail to learn. We must remember that fear and division are political power moves. We must see our shared humanity and listen, really listen for the truth that is found across cultural and ethnic backgrounds and experience."

INNOVATION

DEFINITION OF INNOVATION	Unlocking an environment to create "out of the box" approaches. Offer varied experiences and perspectives in order to fully contribute. Utilized to drive value creation, new ideas, new methods, and better solutions.
POLAR OPPOSITE OF INNOVATION	Organizations that are doing the same thing, stuck in a rut, not willing to change, and clinging to traditional approaches. Nothing stifles innovation faster than indifference, which lies at the other end of the spectrum of innovation. Indifference is the polar opposite of innovation. Lead to higher attrition, dissatisfaction and low engagement due to the lack of opportunity to participate fully in the work environment.
LEVERAGE INNOVATION	Leverage innovation by engaging all of the diversity which fosters more creativity.
EXERIENCE INNOVATION	Experience innovation by setting up an ongoing process and taking that process or tool that seems meaningless and making it an added value because diversity input was at the center of the process for the betterment of all.
DEVELOP INNOVATION	Develop innovation not only by thinking outside the box but by taking the box and throwing it away. Focused on bringing together creative ideas and perspectives that ignite diversity.
WAYS TO CULTIVATE INNOVATION	• Superhero Mission Statement • Yan Koloba Game by Dr. Emmanuel Ngomsi • Connect the 9 Dot Activity

In summary, as a superhero, Tammy brings daring to the table to advance the understanding of innovation. What will you bring to the table to advance innovative efforts in programs and services in the workplace? What cape will you wear when you develop daring programs and services for innovation? In the final chapter, the author will share additional resources that can cultivate Bold Innovation for Greatness.

- Innovation should be leveraged for greater impact in organizations with diverse programs and services.
- Innovation is all about engaging the diversity of the workforce for greater creativity and success.
- Diversity fosters a more creative and innovative workforce.
- Diverse employees need innovative programs and services that offer varied experiences and perspectives in order to fully leverage and contribute in the workplace.
- Diversity is critical for an organizations ability to innovate and adapt in a fast-growing environment.

BIG (CULTURAL) INTELLIGENCE

"We need to recognize and capitalize on the advantages of developing and using cultural proficiency more now than ever before,"

—**Kirk Perucca**

Leveraging Cultural Intelligence

The sixth and final BIG "I" that the author believes allows for a comprehensive fresh perspective is leveraging and embracing cultural intelligence (CQ) with individuals and organizations. Leveraging differences in the workplace through cultural intelligence is a mechanism for great change. According to the research, it is human nature to think, feel, and act from one's own experiences, especially when confronted with differences in the workplace. Cultural Intelligence has been defined in many ways, including the capacity for knowledge, understanding, and self-awareness through engaging and interacting across cultures with individuals who are different from you in the workplace. Cultural Intelligence is a newer diversity level developed years ago by Christopher Earley and Elaine Mosakowski. It can be more generally described as the ability to perceive or infer culturally diverse information and to retain it as knowledge to be applied toward situations and assignments within a work environment. Over time, if leveraged correctly, it will give us the ability to adapt oneself to facilitate effective interactions across cultures to gain new insight and develop better initiatives in the workplace.

The opposite of cultural intelligence is non-culture or an unenlightening environment. Over time, we will not be able to develop relationships beyond our immediate, familiar circle, thus preventing us from benefitting from learning from others. One's personal and professional growth will be stunted.

Experiencing Cultural Intelligence

Bold Intelligence for Greatness is the ability to experience an environment designed to support a better decision-making infrastructure. Diversity and inclusion within an organization broadens an organization's functional perspective within the environment it operates in, whereas cultural intelligence helps to provide valuable insight on both internal and external cultural issues. This experience has the potential of impacting diverse employees with measurable success such as greater equity and growth. Cultural Intelligence has a strong dependency on inclusion. It is important for an organization to incorporate an ideal skillset that works across cultures. All told, the author had the opportunity to experience different cultures and communities starting at a very young age. Whether it was for her family or moving for career opportunities to different communities or for family vacations to different countries, she successfully navigated language, customs, and the like. She learned the importance of engaging authentically with people of different backgrounds and demographics — gaining increased confidence with each journey and increasing her cultural intelligence along the way.

> *Understanding and respect for other cultures/diverse backgrounds. Celebrate those cultural differences on many levels.*
>
> **— T.J. Shelton**
> **Sr. Associate Athletics Director**

Over the past 15 years, organizations have started to include and address CQ in their diversity strategy. Cultural Intelligence (CQ) picks up where emotional intelligence leaves off. According to the author, CQ understanding is at the greatness level. It's about your ability to adapt in order to facilitate effective interactions with individuals who are different from you. And it's about the actions you take to prepare yourself to adapt to those

> *Cultural Intelligence is the ability to understand and competently work with diverse groups or individuals.*
>
> **— Greg Valdovino**
> **Director of Diversity**

environments — reading books, watching movies, attending fairs and festivals, hanging out with different people.

Developing (Cultural) Intelligence

Over the years, two resources have been found useful in helping others understand and increase their knowledge about cultural intelligence. The first one is an article in the *Harvard Business Review* titled "Cultural Intelligence," by Christopher Earley and Elaine Mosakowski (2004). This article has an effective self-assessment for individuals or organizations to utilize as they build their behaviors and positions in this area. In addition, it discusses how one's head, body, and heart must work together to move the needle with cultural intelligence. It references the need to develop confidence overtime to become truly effective with CQ. The second great development approach that has been found effective over the years is the work of Kirk Perucca on the cultural continuum and cultural-proficiency resources and tools. Perucca stated, "We must hold on to the idea that we have the opportunity to 'do better,' recognizing that there is an economic advantage to being 'better together.'"

We can use the economic reality (benefits) of (cultural intelligence), in this case, the practical application of (cultural proficiency) to further the moral imperative that we are compelled to confront. Let's look at a superhero story of how one diversity champion leverages, experiences, develops, and cultivates cultural intelligence.

> *To relate and work effectively across cultures.*
>
> **— Debbie Bass**
> **Vice President**

Kirk displays an amazing ability to interact and then leverage cultural intelligence throughout his work. Kirk Perucca has spent the past 8 years as the President/CEO of Project Equality, a nonprofit organization located in Kansas City that promotes diversity through awareness and skill building through the lens of equality and justice in the workplace. Kirk works to bring corporate, nonprofit, educational, and religious communities together as a force for equality, justice, and fairness in the workplace. Through facilitated discussions community leaders identify and establish best practices that enhance workplace fairness. Project Equality is a program of Kirk Perucca Associates that examines all aspects of diversity and inclusion. Over the past 30 years, Perucca has provided diversity and cultural-competency training for nonprofit organizations, fire and police departments, and major corporations across the nation.

BIG Cultural Intelligence Story

Kirk Perucca is the President and CEO of Project Equality. A principal outcome is working collaboratively to spotlight the best resources in our region that empower fairness in the workplace. The workplace should be a place where employees can thrive and grow. Discrimination is still common in the workplace. It takes many forms: disparate treatment due to race, sexual harassment toward employees, reprisals because of sexual orientation, terminations due to age, ability/disability, or religious bias. Project Equality works to raise the awareness of all forms of discrimination. Kirk Perucca has spent his life educating businesses and nonprofit agencies about diversity and inclusion. As a Presbyterian minister, Perucca serves an urban neighborhood church, with a multicultural congregation. The church is located in a Kansas City neighborhood challenged by racial and economic disparity, diversity, and equality issues. He had also been fortunate to work on diversity and inclusion initiatives with a wide variety of organizations, including area school districts and police departments, Jackson County Sheriff's Department, metropolitan municipalities, corporations, and chambers of commerce. Based on his big impact in the greater Kansas City community, Kirk can be best characterized as a good-natured superhero for diversity and inclusion. His life's work is about "opening up" and, as such, he operates with the conviction of how we work is as important as what we do, and his work ethic is one of a collaborative, respectful, collegial, caring way that enables him to really hear the voices of others that have been impacted by injustice. Perucca's chief goal is to help make people and organizations more Culturally Intelligent related to diversity. This conviction stems from the profound impact of reading the book Man Child in the Promised Land by Claude Brown, in 1968 at 13 years old had on him as the United States began to confront the outcry of injustice from the Civil War that manifested in the Civil Rights movement. The reading and the environment served to open Kirk's eyes to a different reality and years later through his appointments within the Presbyterian church. His good nature and deep convictions led him to become active in Civil Rights — being and staying "woke" long before it became today's mantra to injustice, unfair treatment, women's rights, and, later, LGBQT equality.

On his journey, Kirk Perucca has developed a phenomenal cultural-proficiency scale that he shares as his best practice diversity approach. Over the years, more than 2500 individuals have utilized this tool to build capacity on their cultural intelligence journey. His concept helps make people and organizations become more culturally intelligent. Perucca shared that his scale is based on the model of cultural competency originally developed by Native American Terry Cross in 1988. This model was designed to help individuals and organizations work more effectively with each other and to honor all cultures. The concept uses an inside-out approach in that it requires the individual (and organizations) to answer the question, "How do I show up?" when interacting with other people. According to Perucca, "When one navigates others, particularly those who are different from you, they should go through a process to reflect on "Am I in a learning mode, understanding mode, approachable mode or encouraging mode?" This is significant due to the social, psychological, and economic impact on others in the workplace, communities, and marketplace." "We need to recognize and capitalize on the advantages of developing and using cultural proficiency more now than ever before," Perucca says.

The concept of cultural proficiency is rooted in understanding that examining one's self first is key to opening opportunities. It also recognizes that this is hard work and that there are biases that must be confronted in order to be successful in advancing to the next level. A great analogy is thinking of bias in the United States as a boulder. Let's call it the "bias boulder." It's a big boulder, where there are positive workers on one side chipping away at the structural tenets that support biases. However, on the other side, there are forces and/or group behaviors (sometimes operating with good intentions but resulting in unintentional consequences) that reinforce structural practices and processes. When cultural-proficiency practices are taught, groups can evaluate where they are on the continuum (scale) and begin the work of dismantling destructive practices and replacing them with culturally appropriate behaviors. The process works because it employs a collaborative approach where everyone works together to move along or up the continuum together on an area or issue — not the game where one demographic or ethnic group shoulders the burden for the current state of affairs. Individuals' values are highlighted to demonstrate that there are commonalities among everyone. For instance, everyone values a safe and productive environment — so let's all go to work to build that and take care to incorporate the foundational values of the various populations and cultures affected. Cultural proficiency is significant because one of the first steps is to determine where you are on the cultural continuum. We all live in our own cultural groups — in those groups, we don't notice that it works. Outside of our groups, we notice differences: color, ethnicity, dress, hair, etc. That causes glitches all the time — we expect others to adapt and do not pause to recognize the richness of other groups. We must shift to an inside-out approach where I look at my culture and history and am aware of how I show up, how I come across. In doing so, I listen more, talk less in order to learn about the person. And I show up in a big way — as welcoming, including, and learning, moving away from tunnel vision.

As organizations retool engagement programs and services for success, these six stages must be a part of those future programs. The stages are:

- Cultural Destruction — see differences and stamp them out
- Cultural Incapacity — see differences as wrong and focus on making them conform
- Cultural Blindness — see differences and choose to ignore them

- Cultural Pre-Competency — see differences but respond inappropriately
- Cultural Competency — see differences and respond appropriately
- Cultural Proficiency — see differences and respond and affirm those differences in a variety of ways and across a variety of environments — Institutionalized Concept

Diligent application of this process that steps through these stages results in BIG take-aways for Cultural Intelligence for diversity and inclusion practitioners:

- We learn to embrace the richness of other cultures
- We learn the importance and benefits of navigating other cultures
- We learn to capture the brilliance of others

The BIG book provides us with renewed HOPE. Hope that we can effectively confront and dismantle practices of the past, particularly as they relate to equity, equality, and justice for all. This BIG book provides effective thoughts, resources, and action plans for readers regardless of where they are on the continuum — you can start where you are and grow from there.

INTELLIGENCE (CULTURAL, CQ)

DEFINITION OF CULTURAL INTELLIGENCE	Engaging and interacting across cultures with individuals who are different from you in the workplace (in diverse programs and services). Over time, if leveraged correctly, it will enable us to adapt ourselves to facilitate effective interactions across cultures to gain new insight and develop better initiatives in the workplace.
POLAR OPPOSITE OF CQ	The opposite of Cultural Intelligence is non-culture or living an unenlightened life. We choose instead to live in a vacuum that is void of exposure or experience with other environments or cultures. We limit our ability to walk in the shoes of others or empathize with conditions or issues that are outside of our own cultural context. Over time, we will not be able to develop relationships beyond our immediate, familiar circle, thus preventing us from benefitting from learning from others. Personal and professional growth will be stunted.
LEVERAGE CQ	We leverage Cultural Intelligence (CQ) by wanting to change through sensitivity, adaptability, and learning to embrace a diverse cultural heritage that is rewarding, inspiring, and empowering.
EXERIENCE CQ	We experience cultural intelligence through exposure and experiences in other environments and with other cultures that take us out of our "comfort zone." We have a deep appreciation for differences and are comfort-able with un-comfortable situations that tap into our curiosity and stretch our ability to go beyond our boundaries.
DEVELOP CQ	We develop cultural intelligence through exploration and immersion in other environments, other cultures, other customs and traditions. We are open to enriching our own experience base by connecting with others we may not have previously been associated with. We operate with a courageous spirit that boldly and deliberately steps into other worlds, and we are the better for it.
WAYS TO CULTIVATE CQ	• Cultural Proficiency Scale • Assessing My Life Experiences Assessment • CQ Assessment • Yan Koloba Game • Triangle Chart—EEO • Village 100

In summary, as a superhero, Kirk Perucca brings good nature to the table and advances understanding of Cultural Intelligence (CQ). What will you bring to the table to advance CQ programs and services in the workplace? What cape will you wear when you develop good nature CQ programs and services for success? In the final chapter, the author will share additional resources created by Kirk Perucca that can cultivate Bold Intelligence for Greatness.

- Leveraging and embracing CQ allows for a comprehensive, fresh perspective.
- Cultural Intelligence has a strong dependency on inclusion.
- CQ picks up where emotional intelligence leaves off.
- To be effective with CQ, you need to leverage your head, body, and heart to move the needle.

PART FIVE

The Future BIG Destination

"History and data have proven that having a diverse workforce, a diverse culture, and a diverse community does not mean that they're included or they're interconnected. Inclusion is making sure you have a mix of individuals and you make that mix work — ensuring that all have a voice at the table and the same advantages as others—equality, equity, and justice."

— **Dr. Andrea Hendricks**

For organizations to develop superpowers for this future destination, ongoing change and an effective process must be embraced when it comes to diversity and inclusion work. This work is a "journey not a sprint." It can be a lonely and difficult journey as a superhero/shero human resources or diversity leader to take on the quest to cultivate BIG opportunities in the workplace. You have to cultivate daring, courageous, motivated, epic, and insightful programs and services like the superhero/sheroes highlighted in this book. The past state or the lack of diversity efforts in some organizations cannot be allowed to override the future destination of this BIG framework. Despite where this book will land in your life, it will give you a spark to continue the diversity champions' movement by taking the bold steps that leads to greatness. The bold step begins with a step on the trail, that leads to a lane, to a road, and eventually to that BIG future destination.

In this final chapter, the author will highlight the fourth approach for all six "I's" — the capability to cultivate BIG across programs and services. When you have leveraged, experienced, and developed BIG — all together — individuals or organizations should be ready to change behavior and navigate to cultivating greater diversity and inclusion actions or efforts. To recap some of the key research impacting this work:

- The United States will no longer have any single ethnic or racial majorities by the year 2065. (Pew).
- For every 10% increase in the rate of racial and ethnic diversity on senior executive teams, EBIT rises 0.8%. (McKinsey).
- Ethnically diverse companies are 35% more likely to outperform their respective national industry medians. (McKinsey).
- Gender-diverse companies are 15% more likely to outperform their respective national industry medians. (McKinsey).
- Companies reporting highest levels of racial diversity in their organizations bring in nearly 15 times more sales revenue than those with lowest levels of racial diversity. (*American Sociological Review*)
- 67% of job seekers said a diverse workforce is important when considering job offers. (Glassdoor).

Learning about diversity can be an exciting step in the right direction if individuals and organizations value the journey that is needed to get to the future destination. However, beginning to discuss the topic of diversity can be difficult. Therefore, this section will provide tools, resources, and activities that the author leveraged and experienced while she cultivated her diversity and inclusion journey over the past 25 years in order to reach the future destination of great diversity and inclusion work.

During the first cultivation step, the author developed a super-shero mission statement and a diversity story vision board. She found this very helpful as she began her journey toward BIG. Individuals or organizations who tell their story around diversity and inclusion by writing a superhero/shero diversity mission statement or creating a diversity vision board have taken a critical first step on moving the needle on this journey. This process always starts with your personal commitment to making a difference as a leader or organization. Another great step is connecting with other diversity stories or fables that can communicate a profound message on the BIG journey. Over the past 25 years, Hendricks has several favorite stories/fables from other authors and thought leaders that are mentioned in this book. Two of her favorite fables are: The giraffe and elephant fable in the book titled Building a House for Diversity that was mentioned in an earlier section of this book and the other short fable is about a boy on the beach throwing starfish back in the ocean one at a time. The story is about an elderly man who was walking on the beach one morning and sees a little boy on the beach throwing items in the ocean. The elderly man noticed there were hundreds of starfish. on the beach. He walks up to the little boy and asks the boy why he was throwing one starfish at a time back into the ocean and indicated that it would take him a long time to get all starfish back in the ocean if he only threw back one at a time. The boy replied, "I am throwing one back at a time because it matters to that one." So, individuals and organizations doing this work have to find their diversity story first and invest the time, talent, and resources to move the needle — it matters to that employee, the organization and the community at large—just like the starfish and the elephant.

Let's look at other resources that the author has found to be profound additions to her work over the years. Hendricks suggests individuals or organizations that are ready to cultivate BIG with the six "I's" should consider utilizing existing resources right out of the box in order to launch or leverage more quickly and effectively. Oftentimes, organizations are spending too much time trying to customize the work to their environments and miss the opportunities to move the needle with diverse programs and services because they do not leverage great work already cultivated for success. According to Hendricks, "It is important to remove the roadblocks that prevent you or the organizations for developing diverse programs and services. It is important to create a healthy and safe environment through the use of great diversity awareness tools, books, and easy activities. When an organization readily introduces employees to tools that are required beyond their individual role, that individual has the opportunity to grasp the fact that the end result depends on them fulfilling their role or business obligation. This awareness helps employees understand that other diversity elements and engagements depend on their understanding how their performance and engagement with others directly impacts the organization's potential for greatness.

The BIG Cultivation

The author has spent over 25 years looking at what would be great practices to reach the B.I.G. framework for success. Those best practices for cultivating diversity and inclusion programs and services/efforts in the workplace are:

- Acknowledge major holidays of all cultures even if you don't offer time off.
- Address bias in the workplace.
- Attend diversity workshops and seminars.
- Assist diverse communities in your footprint to be as successful as possible.
- Consider gender neutral language for key areas within your organization.
- Corporate partnerships and sponsorships with diverse organizations, universities and communities.
- Create a welcoming culturally relevant environment.
- Create required diverse slates for leadership roles.
- Develop a comprehensive diversity strategy.
- Develop effective diversity practices and policies.
- Develop several employee/business programs and networks to support employees from all backgrounds.
- Ensure diversity questions are a part of employee engagement surveys.
- Ensure interview committee/process has diverse representation.
- Hire a full time diversity executive/officer/leader to drive efforts.
- Internal recognition for employees who champion diversity.
- Launch Mentorship and Sponsorship programs.

- Let leaders and associates tell stories of their diversity engagement and commitments.
- Leverage diversity benchmark data, research and information.
- Measure meaningful impact goals.
- Offer pipeline, academy and rotational programs and experiences to help diversify the workplace.
- Open conversations about diversity and inclusion in the workplace.
- Performance discussions and results should include diversity goals and metrics.
- Recognition for diversity efforts on diversity indexes/surveys.
- Robust diversity and inclusion training and development programs.
- Seamlessly embed diversity into all areas of the organization. Not only within HR programs.
- Visibility on diversity in your community.

BIG Resources Chart

Name of Resource	Author or Creator/Inspired By
On Common Ground Activity Explore differences and commonalities. The purpose is to help create awareness about the differences and commonalities present within groups/teams/organizations. Related to Inclusion, Interactions, Intersectionality	This activity is a simple way to get people connected together. There are several on common ground icebreakers and activities found online.
Assessing My Life Experiences Self-Assessment Tool. Assess how multicultural your different life experiences have been. Related to Inclusion and Intelligence.	Developed by Dr. Barbara Love, University of Massachusetts, Amherst and Dr. Don Bratchers, Georgia Institute of Technology
Cultural Intelligence (CQ) Assessment. Measures an individual's capability for working and relating across cultures. Related to Inclusion, Interactions, Intersectionality, Intelligence.	Cultural Intelligence article and assessment by P. Christopher Earley and Elaine Mosakowski Harvard Business Review October 2004

Name of Resource	Author or Creator/Inspired By
Social Networks Articles and Information. Ability to see the complex web of diverse connections between people in and beyond your organization. Related to Interactions.	Developing Network Perspecive by Cullen, Palus and Appaneal. Center for Creative Leadership https://www.iedp.com/providers/ccl-center-for-creative-leadership-ccl/
The Leader Network Diagnostic (LND) – The Network Tool. Practical and comprehensive tool for leaders to use in order to quickly examine the effectiveness of their social network. Related to Interactions.	http://www.leadernetworkdiagnostic.com/
Personal Board of Directors. Everyone needs a team of people—Personal Board of Directors (PBD) who can provide support for their thought leadership journey. A group of people you consult regularly to get advice and feedback. Related to Interactions and Ideas.	https://www.google.com Search, Personal Board of Directors
Yan Koloba Game Team building game which reaches across all cultural boundaries and engages the players in an exercise that teaches character traits such as respect, unity, tolerance, trust, all in a FUN environment. Related to Interactions, Inclusion, (cultural) Intelligence.	Dr. Emmanuel Ngomsi ALL WORLD LANGUAGES & CULTURES, INC. http://www.universalhighways.com

Name of Resource	Author or Creator/Inspired By
Diversity Dimensions Wheel Understanding that each individual is unique and recognizing your individual differences. These can be along, the dimensions of race, ethnicity, gender, sexual orientation, socio-economic status, age, physical abilities, religious beliefs, political beliefs, or other ideologies. Related to Inclusión, Interactions, Ideas, Innovation, Intelligence, Intersectionality	https://community.astc.org/ ccli/resources-for-action/ group-activities/diversity-wheel Also adapted from Loden & Rosener. Workforce America: Managing Employee Diversity as a Vital Resource. McGraw-Hill1990.
The Iceberg The iceberg is a fitting metaphor for diversity. Nine-tenths of an iceberg resides below the surface. Just as it is difficult to judge the size and shape of an iceberg, it is also difficult to ascertain all of an individual's diversity traits simplify looking at them or attempting to guess based upon observations or other perceptions. Related to Inclusion, Intersectionality	Beyond the Tip of the Iceberg: Five Stages Toward Cultural Competence. Jerome Hanley
Thought Revolution Exercises How to unlock your inner genius—learn to think differently to be effective. Related to Ideas Innovation	William Donius: developer of the unique methodology. **Thought Revolution.** The book is about breaking through complacent, conventional thinking to think differently about the problems faced in life.

Name of Resource	Author or Creator/Inspired By
Four Quadrants of Wellbeing. How small changes can make BIG Shifts. There is a crossover—inter-dependence—to becoming well. Related to Interactions, Innovation	Dr. Michelle Robin—author and founder of Your Wellness Connection. https://www.drmichellerobin.com/
Respect Poster An activity to allow participants to explore what respect means in the workplace. In addition, equips employees at every level to broaden their definition of diversity and build positive, productive relationships. Powerful demonstration of what to say and do when cultural differences impact jobs and working relationships. Related to Inclusion, Interactions	Just Be F.A.I.R. Training
Building A House Fable A fable about a giraffe and an elephant. They consider themselves friends. But when the giraffe invites the elephant into his home, disaster strikes. The house has been designed to meet the needs of the tall, slender giraffe. Related to Inclusion, Interactions, Ideas, Intelligence	Author Roosevelt Thomas, Jr Building A House for Diversity Book. He was often referred to as the "father of diversity," was the founder of the American Institute for Managing Diversity Inc.

Name of Resource	Author or Creator/Inspired By
What's In A Name Icebreaker Activity Share the story of where your name comes from and what your name means. Everyone's name has a surprisingly interesting origin. Helps to build intercultural respect and understanding. Related to Intelligence, Intersectionality	
Head, Heart, Body Example. Three sources of cultural intelligence. Related to Interaction, Intelligence.	Cultural Intelligence Article P. Christopher Earley and Elaine MosakowskiHarvard Business Review October 2004
TMAY-Tell Me About Yourself Icebreaker The "Tell Me About Yourself" process is one of the most notoriously open-ended interview questions or get to know another person around. Related to Interactions, Intelligence	
Tolerance Scale Activity How people respond to others in terms of their attitudes toward differences.	ProGroup. *Attitudes Toward Differences*. Minneapolis, MN: The Professional Development Group, Inc., 1993-1999. Discusses behaviors and the impact of biases and assumptions. An excellent resource for any area of the organization,

Name of Resource	Author or Creator/Inspired By
The participants getting a mental snapshot of people with whom they enjoy working with and people with whom they have trouble working with daily and participants do some analysis about what might be behind the choices they make. Related to Inclusion, Interactions.	One Main Street S.E., Ste. 200 Minneapolis, MN 55414 800/651-4093 progroup@progroupinc.com http://www.lacrosseconsortium.org/uploads/content_files/Tolerance_Scale_without_questions.pdf
Survey of Hopefulness Establishes a baseline of perspectives and biases that helps individuals understand their whole self, related to problem solving and issue resolution. Understand how life experiences shape our thoughts, reactions, expectations, and approaches to problem solving. Related to Intersectionality.	Dr. Karen Boyd kpboyd5056@sbcglobal.net
Superhero Mission Statement Build your own mission statement for diversity and inclusion. Whaat type of Superhero for justice are you?. Related to all of the "I's"	Do a search and look up how others created their statements through the images and words
IRAC Methodology Standard of legal writing structured to communicate logical reasoning in a precise fashion. Related to Interactions	Laura Isabel Law School Best Practice https://opinionfront.com/explanation-of-irac-method-of-legal-reasoning-with-examples

Name of Resource	Author or Creator/Inspired By
Vision Board Tool A vision board is a tool used to help clarify, concentrate and maintain focus on a specific goal. Literally, a vision board is any sort of board on which you display images that represent whatever you want to be, do or have in your life. Related to all of the "I's".	Do a search and look up how others created their statements through the images and words
Circles of My Multicultural Self Activity Many things make up your identity. Related to Intersectionality, Intelligence.	diversityactivities-resource-guide.pdf
Diversity Bingo To help the people know more about each other's diverse backgrounds. Related to all "I's".	diversityactivities-resource-guide.pdf
Village 100 Activity Intended to inspire thought regarding the diversity within our world and the need for tolerance and understanding. Related to Intelligence.	https://www.media-partners.com/diversity/village_of_100.htm

Name of Resource	Author or Creator/Inspired By
Connect The Dot Activity To demonstrate that we often limit our perspective and choices. Related to Ideas, Innovation	From Casse, Pierre. Training for the cross-cultural mind: A handbook for cross-cultural trainers and consultants. 2nd edition. Washington, D.C.: The Society for Intercultural Education, Training, and Research, 1981. http://nwlink.com/~donclark/leader/diverse2.html
Your Tool Kit for Success: The Professional Woman's Guide for Advancing to the C-Suite Book The book sets out to teach women of every race, culture, background, and affinity group how to become passionate leaders who can not only expand their own careers but also enhance the businesses they will ultimately lead. Lead by Example, Sheila Robinson's book on leadership development in the 21st century is a moving memoir and no-nonsense guide to how to succeed in the complex culture of today's corporate America.	Dr. Sheila Robinson
Crossing the Line Knowing and Communicating Personal Value around diversity. Related to Inclusion	diversityactivities-resource-guide.pdf

Name of Resource	Author or Creator/Inspired By
Harvard IAT Online Assessment— Project Implicit Demonstrates the conscious-unconscious divergences/bias self-assessment This new method is called the Implicit Association Test, or IAT. Your willingness to examine your own possible biases is an important step in understanding the roots of stereotypes and prejudice in our society.	https://implicit.harvard.edu/ implicit/takeatest.html
The Seat Book The Seat: How to Get Invited to the Table When You're Over-Performing and Undervalued."	Dr. Shirley Davis https://drshirleydavis.com/tag/ the-seat/
Deep See Products We enable individuals and organizations to see beyond the surface, to see clearly for themselves the rich opportunities—and challenges—of today's multigenerational, multicultural workplace and the new competencies that today's leaders require. Related to all "I's".	https://www.deepseeconsulting. com
The Herman Grid To discover that first impressions. Related to Interaction, Intersectionality	From Casse, Pierre. Training for the cross-cultural mind: A handbook for cross-cultural trainers and consultants. 2nd edition. Washington, D.C.: The Society for Intercultural Education, Training, and Research, 1981.

Name of Resource	Author or Creator/Inspired By
Confronting the Black Swan: A Case Study of Corporate Learning Master's thesis exploring corporate learning using the theory of organizational knowledge creation to understand how social practices and leadership behaviors affect employee knowledge and beliefs and thus the implications for a firm's knowledge creation.	Tammy Broaddus https://kuscholarworks.ku.edu/bitstream/handle/1808/14771/Broaddus_ku_0099M_13127_DATA_1.pdf?sequence=1&isAllowed=y
Cultural Profciency Scale A tool that helps make people and organizations more intelligent related to cultural characteristics, customs and their implications. Related to Intelligence (cultural).	Kirk Perucca http://kperuccaassociates.com/
Book: Wisdom of the Crowds Champions the aggregation of information in groups, resulting in decisions that, he argues, are often better than could have been made by any single member of the group. Related to all "I's".	James Surowieck, Author

The integrated framework starts with a key superpower ingredient in order to get to the future destination, and that is one must embrace intersectionality. It is here that organizations must be willing to allow an employee to bring their whole self to work and reduce the social biases by tackling both negative cultural as well as generational perceptions in the workplace. Cultivating diverse interactions in the workplace is the second key superpower ingredient you must pick up along the way on your journey to the destination. It is here that organizations must be willing to explore where the gaps or divisions exist in the lack of cross cultural interactions as it relates to biases, blind spots, or filters. Tara Duggan writes in her article "The Importance of Interaction in Workplace Issues" that when employees are presented with opportunities to share cultural traditions and to participate in role-playing exercises designed to solve problems in a nontraditional way, workers tend to become more tolerant of other viewpoints. Duggan encourages workshops and seminars designed to allow employees an opportunity to practice real-life-based interactions. When addressed in an environment, an employee has a chance to recognize and address their individual attitudes toward culturally diverse backgrounds. The first two superpower ingredients leads to the third one: inclusiveness. If you are not willing to accept people for who they are or to interact with people who are different from you, then you are not going to be authentically inclusive. The act of interacting with one another as unique individuals who have an appreciation for each other's differences can create an all-inclusive work environment. You must first be comfortable in your own skin and then be able to step openly into another's world for understanding and achievement of the greater good. When cultivating diverse ideas, an organization must be willing to hear and entertain ideas that come from more diverse experiences. This requires a deliberate platform designed in every program and service to exchange ideas. If this is cultivated correctly, then it becomes seamlessly embedded in the learning culture and you have sparked the fourth superpower ingredient. It feels natural and will spark more greatness along the journey. Each instance of exchange will bring similar experiences. However, each employee should be encouraged to incorporate a new sense of "readiness" to hear diverse ideas. When something is approached with expectation, there is an inherent effort made to not only hear a diverse idea or perspective, but a tendency to explore the idea from a new and often unfamiliar point of view. This creates a sense of inclusion and value among all employees. In his latest book, *The Success Factor: How Smart Leaders Deliver Outstanding Value*, Andrew Kakabadse, professor of governance and strategic leadership at Henley Business School in the UK, shares that critical to smart leaders creating value and delivering success is the power of "diversity of thinking" — the capacity of theory to seek out and reckon with multiple points of view and, based upon the knowledge gained, act in a systematic repeatable fashion. Kakabadse derived insights from interviews with senior managers from more than 100 organizations in 14 countries. Kakabadse indicates that, for organizations to differentiate themselves from other organizations — diversity thinking, ideas, perspectives are integral to value deliver and must be embedded into the culture. Since we already discussed the role inclusion and interaction play in attaining great diversity, let's shift attention specifically to the fifth superpower ingredient—innovation. The Civil Rights Movement, Affirmative Action, and gender-sensitive legislation have all forced human resource departments to create the image of inclusion. Today, we are more likely to see a diverse global representation throughout companies that aim for the monetary benefits that come from an appearance of diversity through well-thought-out marketing plans. However, the truth of a company's real commitment to diversity is often exposed in the boardrooms and at the leadership levels where decisions are made on how to move a company forward. In the realm of "true" diversity, stakeholders are willing to consider innovative accessibility and cultural intelligence over profitability—which is the sixth and future superpower ingredient on this journey. A diverse organization accepts diverse perspectives that are considered without immediate dismissal based on preconceived stereotypes, ethnic bias, or cultural association, which cultivates an intellectually cul- turally (CQ) engaged diverse environment.

Organizations have found that inclusive interactions can often lead to innovative outcomes including high retention rates, extraor- dinary growth, and great profits. When an organization understands that by inviting the "whole" person, in all of their diversity, to par- ticipate, it becomes an advocate for intellectual intelligence and opens the door to greatness. Organizations must "innovate or die," according to Bill Gates. In a 2014 survey of 1500 executives, three- quarters said that innovation was among their company's top three priorities. In the survey, the executives stated that diverse ideas is a key breakthrough for gaining innovation. Diversity of thinking is gaining prominence as a strategy for new insights and will be critical to success. In the end, you must be willing to journey forward until you reach anything that resembles a glimpse of what you envisioned. Diversity doesn't guarantee inclusion, diverse interactions or ideas, cultural intelligence or innovation unless relativity can develop dur- ing the process of cultivating one's vision of greatness. This is where you boldly develop effective BIG approaches toward your future destination. The author focused her attention on this book on the six major frameworks that address issues challenges of creating a diverse and inclusive workplace. This BIG approach suggests that diversity and HR leaders must take bold steps to address the next level to close those gaps for diverse college students and employees as mentioned at the beginning of this book.

The responsibility does not just fall on the diversity and HR lead- ers. Everyone must do their part—leaders and managers, employ- ees. The author hopes each person is motivated in the organization to leverage, experience, develop and cultivate all six frameworks imme- diately. She hopes that the ideas, stories, and resources presented throughout the book will spur new and more effective actions. The primary area for organizations and leaders focused on driving diversity is whether our actions – (what we are doing) are in alignment with our beliefs – (what we value). We have to remove the barriers that are preventing us from achieving BIG before the next 50 years. She believes there are numerous positive stories and examples of great work around the country of what is possible for organizations. There is hope for a brighter future. We must press on until we reach the future destination desired state.

Write your diversity mission statement:

1. What does diversity mean to you?

2. Write your diversity story?

3. How do you connect with diversity?

4. Why?

5. Write your superhero/shero diversity mission statement?

6. What one word describes your superhero/shero diversity efforts that you would write on your cape?

1. _____
2. _____
3. _____
4. _____
5. _____

7. In your own words, define intersectionality. Then, cite an example of how you personally or professionally embrace bold intersectionality efforts for greatness for diverse programs and services in organizations.

8. In your own words, define interactions. Then, cite an example of how you personally or professionally engage with others in bold interactions for greatness through diverse programs and services in organizations.

9. In your own words, define diverse ideas/perspectives. Then, cite an example of how you personally or professionally leverage bold diverse ideas/perspectives for greatness through diverse programs and services in organizations.

10. In your own words, define inclusion. Then, cite an example of how you personally or professionally deliver bold inclusive efforts for greatness through diverse programs and services in organizations.

11. In your own words, define innovation. Then, cite an example of how you personally professionally advance diversity through bold innovative efforts for greatness through diverse programs and services in organizations.

12. In your own words, define cultural intelligence. Then, cite an example of how you personally or professionally utilize bold cultural intelligence for greatness through diverse programs and services in organizations.

13. The BIG "I's". How have you leveraged, experienced, developed, cultivated each "I"? Assess your engagement with each "I". Use the chart on the next page to complete this exercise.

   a. In column a, check the "I's" that you leverage well—personally or professionally-related to diversity.

   b. In column b, check the "I's" that you need to develop—personally or professionally related to diversity.

   c. In column c, identify resources that can assist you to leverage that "I" for greater effectiveness.

	a	b	c
Intersectionality			
Interactions			
Ideas– diverse			
Inclusion			
Innovation			
Intelligence– Cultural			

Dr. Andrea Hendricks

14. Create a diversity and inclusion vision board (future state for you or your organization).

15. Your BIG Journey Action Plan—One Year. Two Years. What will you do to move the needle toward the future destination?

3 months	
6 months	
9 months	
12 months	
18 months	
2 years	

It is my greatest hope that this book has inspired employees, leaders or organizations to become more aware of behavior patterns that are keeping you stuck in a rut and that one can trade those habits for the BIG superpower ingrdients and rituals that are aligned with your overall diversity vision, mission and purpose. This journey does not happen overnight, and hopefully this book will be a spark for your amazing future diversity journey.

The cultivating phase offers a way to put some of what you have read into action. Here's an opportunity to reflect on what aspects of this book apply most to your current diversity journey so that you or your organization can start planning for future productive behavior.

Let's recap the BIG Journey:

• You must have a spark of interest and passion for this work.

• It is a personal journey not a sprint.

• Be willing to understand the history of race and diversity in America. This will allow you to look at diversity in America through a broader lens.

• Diversity is not the same as inclusion.

• Be willing to expand to different approaches to increase capacity to meet the needs of diverse employees.

• An effective process must be embraced when it comes to diversity and inclusion work.

PART SIX

Bibliography

Anand, Rohini. (26 February 2013). How Diversity and Inclusion Drive Employee Engagement

Astin, Alexander W. (1 June 1982) *Minorities in American Higher Education: Recent Trends, Current*

Prospects and Recommendations (Jossey Bass Higher & Adult Education Series). Jossey-Bass Inc., 1st edition.

Barta, Thomas, Markus Kleiner, and Tilo Neumann. (2012 April). Is There Payoff from Top-Team Diversity? *McKinsey Quarterly*. Retrieved from https://www.mckinsey.com/business-functions/organization/our-insights/is-there-a-payoff-from-top-team-diversity.

Chrobot-Mason, Donna. (2003). *Keeping the Promise: Psychological contract violations for minority employees*. Journal of Managerial Psychology, 18. 22–45.

Cohn, D'Vera. (5 October 2015). Future Immigration Will Change the Face of America by 2065. *Numbers, Facts, and Trends Shaping Your World*. Retrieved from http://www.pewresearch.org/fact-tank/2015/10/05/future-immigration-will-change-the-face-of-america-by-2065/

Columbia School of Law. (8 June 2017). Professor Crenshaw coined the term and co-founded the African American Policy Forum. Before AAPF's 20th anniversary, Crenshaw reflects on where intersectionality is heading. *Kimberle Crenshaw on Intersectionality, More than Two Decades Later.* Retrieved from https://www.law.columbia.edu/pt-br/news/2017/06/kimberle-crenshaw-intersectionality.

Comaford, Christine. (2018). *Power Your Tribe: Create Resilient Teams in Turbulent Times.* McGraw-Hill Education.

Davis, Shirley Dr. "The Seat" – Strategies for How to Get it, Keep it, and Create One for Others. *Dr. Shirley Davis, The Success Doctor*, 12 January 2016, https://drshirleydavis.com/the-seat-strategies-for-how-to-get-it-keep-it-and-create-one-for-others/.

Deloitte. "Winning Over the Next Generation of Leaders." The 2016 Deloitte Millennial Survey, 2016.

Dickstein, Morris. (2009). *Dancing in the Dark: A Cultural History of the Great Depression.* New York, New York: W. W. Norton & Company.

DiversityInc. Retrieved from https://www.diversityinc.com/diversity-management/how-diversity-and-inclusion-drives-employee-engagement.

Dobbin Frank and Alexandra Kalev. 2016 July-August. Why Diversity Programs Fail. *Harvard Business Review.* Retrieved from https://hbr.org/2013/12/how-diversity-can- drive-innovation.

Duggan, Tara. (n.d.). How to Develop a Diversity Training Program. *Small Business - Chron.com.* Retrieved from http://smallbusiness.chron.com/develop-diversity-training-program-39904.html

Earley, P. Christopher and Elaine Mosakowski. 2004 October. Cross-Cultural Management: Cultural

Intelligence. Harvard Business Review. Retrieved from https://hbr.org/2004/10/cultural-intelligence.

Forbes Insight. *Global Diversity and Inclusion: Fostering Innovation through a Diverse Workforce.* 11 July 2011. New York, Forbes Insights.

Gallup. Using Employee Engagement to Build a Diverse Workforce. 21 March 2016. Riffkin, Rebecca and Jim Harter. Employee Engagement Gallup Blog. Retrieved from https://news.gallup.com/opinion/gallup/190103/using-employee-engagement-build-diverse-workforce.aspx.

Gender Advisory Council. *The leaking pipeline: Where are our female leaders? 79 women share their Stories.* * 2008 March. PricewaterhouseCoopers.

GlassDoor. "Two-Thirds of People Consider Diversity Important When Deciding Where to Work." Glassdoor Survey, 17 November 2014.

Global Corporate College. "Towards Inclusivity.*" A White Paper on Diversity Best Practice*. Corporate Training White Paper. Maricopa Corporate College. 1 August 2016.

Greenhaus, J., Parasuraman, S., & Wormley, W. (1990). *Effects of Race on Organizational Experiences, Job Performance Evaluations, and Career Outcomes*. The Academy of Management Journal, 33(1), 64-86. Retrieved from http://www.jstor.org/stable/256352

Griswold, Allison. (27 September 2013). Why 'Thought Diversity' Is The Future Of The Workplace Read. Australia: *Business*

Insider. Retrieved from https://www.businessinsider.com.au/the-future-of-workplace-diversity-is-here-2013-9.

Heidrick & Struggles. "Creating a Culture of Mentorship" Heidrick & Struggles International, Inc. Survey, 2017.

Hendricks, Andrea. (1998) *Adult Learners' Level of Satisfaction with Campus Services at a Community College*. Ph. D. dissertation, University Name, database or ID number.

Hewlett, Sylvia Ann, Melinda Marshall, and Laura Sherbin. 2013 December. How Diversity Can Drive Innovation. *Harvard Business Review*. Retrieved from https://hbr.org/2013/12/how-diversity-can-drive-innovation.

Horn, P. W., Roberson, L., & Ellis, A. D. (2008). Challenging Conventional Wisdom about Who Quits: Revelations from Corporate America. Journal of Applied Psychology, 93 (1), 1–34.

Hunt, Vivian, Dennis Layton and Sara Prince. 2014 November. *Diversity Matters*. McKinsey & Company. Retrieved from http://academicanswers.waldenu.edu/faq/73164

Jones, James & Harter, James. (2005). *Race Effects on the Employee Engagement-Turnover Intention Relationship*. Journal of Leadership & Organizational Studies.

Kakabadse, Andrew. (2015). *The Success Formula: How Smart Leaders Deliver Outstanding Value*. Bloomsbury Publishing Plc.

Kerby, Sophia and Crosby Burns. (12 July 2012). *The Top 10 Economic Facts of Diversity in the Workplace*. Center for American Progress.

Larson, Erik. (21 September 2017) New Research: Diversity + Inclusion =. Better Decision Making at Work. *Forbes*. Retrieved from https://www.forbes.com/sites/eriklarson/2017/09/21/new-research-diversity-inclusion-better-decision-making-at-work/#242197ce4cbf

Lerner, Allan W. (1 October 1992) *Continuing Higher Education: The Coming Wave.* New York: Teachers College Printers; New ed. Edition.

Livemore, David. (30 May 2011). *The Cultural Intelligence Difference: Master the One Skill You Can't Do Without in Today's Global Economy.* New York: AMACOM, American Management Association.

Madera, Juan & Dawson, Mary & Guchait, Priyanko. (2016). *Psychological Diversity Climate: Justice, Racioethnic Minority Status and Job Satisfaction.* International Journal of Contemporary Hospitality Management.

Maslow, A.H. (2016). *A Theory of Human Motivation.* Midwest Journal Press.

McLeod, David. (2018). What is Employee Engagement. Retrieved from https://engageforsuccess.org/what-is-employee-engagement

Muir, M. R. and Lin Li. (2014). *What are the top factors that drive employee retention and are there demographic* (gender, generation, ethnicity, geography, etc.) *differences in these factors?* Retrieved 2 December 2018 from Cornell University, ILR School http://digitalcommons.ilr.cornell.edu/student/59

Ngomsi, Emmanuel. (2008). *Shocking Cultures: Hilarious and Disastrous Challenges of Foreign Workers in the U.S.A.* Lee's Summit, Missouri: All World Languages & Cultures, Inc.

Nugent, Julie S., Alixandra Pollack, and Dnika J. Travis. *The Day-to-Day Experiences of Workplace Inclusion and Exclusion.* New York: Catalyst, 2016.

Parsi, Novid. (16 January 2017). Workplace Diversity and Inclusion Gets Innovative. *Society for Human Resource Management.* Retrieved from https://www.shrm.org/hr-today/news/hr-magazine/0217/pages/disrupting-diversity-in-the-workplace.aspx

Rosenberg, M., & McCullough, B. C. (1981). Mattering: Inferred significance and mental health among adolescents. *Research in Community & Mental Health, 2,* 163-182.

Ross, Howard J. (2014). *Everyday Bias: Identifying and Navigating Unconscious Judgement in Our Daily Lives.* Lanham, Maryland: Rowman & Littlefield.

Schlossberg, N., A. Lynch, and A. W. Chickering. (1989). *Improving Higher Education Environments for Adults: Responsive Programs and Services from Entry to Departure.* (Jossey Bass Higher & Adult Education Series). San Francisco : Jossey-Bass, 1989.

Smith, Christie and Stephanie Turner. (2015). *The Radical Transformation of Diversity and Inclusion. The Millennial Influence.* United States: Deloitte Development LLC, 2015. Retrieved from Deloitte University: The Leadership Center for Inclusion website: https://www2.deloitte.com/content/dam/Deloitte/us/Documents/about-deloitte/us-inclus-millennial-influence-120215.pdf.

Surowiecki, James. (2004). *The Wisdom of Crowds.* New York City, New York: Anchor Books.

Talent Culture Team. (14 August 2018). *How to Intentionally Create a More Inclusive Culture.* Talent Culture. Retrieved from https://talentculture.com/how-to-intentionally-create-a-more-inclusive-culture/.

Tencer, Daniel. (2011, September 9). Forbes Survey: Workplace Diversity Key to Innovation. *Huffpost*. Retrieved from https://www.huffingtonpost.ca/2011/07/29/workplace-diversity-innovation_n_913214.html.

Thomas, R. Roosevelt Jr. 1990, March – April. From Affirmative Action to Affirming Diversity. *Harvard Business Review*. Retrieved from https://hbr.org/1990/03/from-affirmative-action-to-affirming-diversity

Toossi, Miltra. (2002 May). *A century of change: the U.S. labor force, 1950–2050*. Monthly Labor Review: Labor Force Change, 1950–2050.

Wadors, Pat. 2016, August 10. Diversity Efforts Fall Short Unless Employees Feel that They Belong. *Harvard Business Review*. Retrieved from https://hbr.org/2016/08/diversity-efforts-fall-short-unless-employees-feel-that-they-belong.

Walter, Ekaterina. (14 January 2014) Reaping the Benefits of Diversity Modern Business Innovation. *Forbes*. Retrieved from https://www.forbes.com/sites/ekaterinawalter/2014/01/14/reaping-the-benefits-of-diversity-for-modern-business-innovation/#30c8b692a8f6.

Wellins, Richard, Paul Bernthal, and Mark Phelps. (2005*). Employee Engagement: The Key to Realizing Competitive Advantage*. Development Dimensions International, Inc. Retrieved from https://www.ddiworld.com/ddi/media/monographs/employeeengagement_mg_ddi.pdf?ext=.pdf

Woods, Susan. (2010). *Thinking about Diversity-Related Conflict: Respect, Recognition and Learning*. Building Working Relationships/Improving Outcomes. New York: Henderson Woods, LLC.

Woolfe, Sylvie. (2017 October). *10 Diversity Hiring Statistics That Will Make You Think. Diversity Hiring.* Retrieved from https://blog.clearcompany.com/10-diversity-hiring-statistics-that-will-make-you-rethink-your-decisions.

US Equal Employment Opportunity Commission. (2014). *2014 Job Patterns for Minorities and Women in Private Industry (EEO-1).* Retrieved from https://www.aaaa.org/wp-content/uploads/2016/05/EEOC-Minorities-women_adv5418.pdf.